Table of Contents

The Jefferson Conspiracy
Some Called It Treason

1

Harlow Giles Unger

About the Author

Harlow Giles Unger is a veteran journalist, broadcaster, educator, and historian. The author of more than 30 books, he is a former Distinguished Visiting Fellow in American History at George Washington's Mount Vernon. The *Washington Post* named him one of America's premier presidential biographers for his best-selling biography of James Monroe—*The Last Founding Father.* He is a graduate of Yale University.

Books by Harlow Giles Unger

John Hancock: Merchant King and American Patriot

Noah Webster: The Life and Times of an American Patriot

Lafayette.

The Unexpected George Washington: His Private Life.

America's Second Revolution

The Last Founding Father: James Monroe and a Nation's Call to Greatness

Lion of Liberty: Patrick Henry and the Call to a New Nation

American Tempest: How the Boston Tea Party Sparked a Revolution

Improbable Patriot: The Secret History of Monsieur de Beaumarchais

John Quincy Adams

John Marshall: The Chief Justice Who Saved the Nation

First Founding Father: Richard Henry Lee and the Call to Independence

Dr. Benjamin Rush: The Founding Father Who Healed a Wounded Nation

Thomas Paine and the Clarion Call for American Independence

Table of Contents

Illustrations

Chapter 1
À la Bastille

In 1784, a year after the United States of America had wrested independence from Britain, Virginia's 41-year-old Thomas Jefferson walked into l'Hôtel de Langeac, a handsome, though unfurnished mansion that he had rented on the corner of rue de Berri and the Champs Elysées in Paris.

He had always dreamed of visiting Paris, and his arrival marked the fulfillment of that dream, along with a chance to visit the rest of France.

More important than seeing the sights of France, was Jefferson's goal of escaping the deep depression that had him contemplating suicide after the death of his 34-year-old wife Martha two years earlier, in 1782.

"I scarcely supposed that his grief could be so violent as to justify his swooning away whenever he sees his children," said his cousin Virginia Attorney General Edmund Randolph. It was Randolph who feared Jefferson would take his own life. Equally fearful relatives took in his three daughters to protect them from what his friend James Madison called a "stupor of mind" that left him "as dead as she was."

Madison was serving in the Continental Congress at the time and urged Jefferson to travel abroad. In the spring of 1785, Franklin's imminent departure from France offered a perfect opportunity, and Madison spurred Congress to appoint him Franklin's replacement. Jefferson leaped at the opportunity to distance himself from the scene of his recent grief.

Charged with establishing trade relations between his country and France and, if possible, other friendly European countries, he searched Paris for a building that would reflect the wealth and power of a major nation.

The Hôtel de Langeac on what was then the western edge of Paris was spacious enough to serve as both his residence and his nation's embassy. To ensure that its elegance matched or surpassed that of other foreign embassies, Jefferson set about furnishing it with the finest furniture, carpets, mirrors, sculptures, paintings, china, and silver he could find to fill the rooms.

Anticipating the need to host elegant official dinners for French government ministers and foreign emissaries, he installed the most modern kitchen equipment. He brought his own cook from his Virginia plantation home—a slave, James Hemings—and he arranged to have Hemings trained in French cuisine to serve the eminent guests the Virginian anticipated receiving.

1. Jefferson's Hôtel de Langeac
on what is now the Champs Elysées at the corner of rue de Berri.

Household slaves were not uncommon in the homes of 18th century Paris. Most had been acquired in French colonies by wealthy planters, colonial administrators, sea captains, and high ranking army officers who had returned to France to retire. France would not abolish slavery until 1845.

Rather than cut off all ties to his family, he arranged for his oldest daughter, 11-year-old Martha (nick-named "Patsy") brought to Paris, accompanied by James Hemings' 14-year-old sister Sally, also a slave. With Patsy enrolled in the prestigious girls' boarding school l'Abbaye Royale de Panthemont—about 5 miles away on the Left Bank—Sally spent most of her time in Paris satisfying Jefferson's personal passions.

After outfitting himself with fashionable French clothes, Jefferson set about living the life of an aristocrat/diplomat, albeit without the noble title that adorned his counterparts from other nations. The United States, after all, was a republic in which Jefferson bore the only acceptable title of "Mister."

2. U. S. Ambassador to France Thomas
Jefferson toured the ruins of Bastille prison.

Despite his status as a commoner, Jefferson re-established friendships he had had with many French aristocrats who had served with the French army in America's War of Independence.

Escorted by men such as the Marquis de Lafayette, Jefferson quickly became a regular in the best Paris "salons," where high-level French government officials, noblemen, artists, and intellectuals shared palace gossip with other officials, noblemen, artists, and intellectuals—and with spies who posed as officials, noblemen, artists, and intellectuals.

What Jefferson did not know—could not know—was that the Foreign Minister Charles Gravier, Comte de Vergennes, continued to believe passionately that "England is our first enemy"—despite the Treaty of Paris that both nations had signed ending their war as well as America's War of Independence.

The primary reason France had granted the Americans so much aid, he admitted privately, was "the enfeeblement of England, by depriving her of one-third of her empire."

Besides the military and financial support France had granted the United States in their War of Independence—more than 140 million livres, or nearly $30 billion today—he had masterminded a scheme "to separate all the English colonies from their mother country forever and prevent any kind of reunion between them."

As it was, however, the United States had already resumed trading with its former oppressor. Instead of allowing France to recoup its investment in the war from American trade, Americans actually increased their trade with Britain. American merchants were simply too used to British goods and the British monetary system and preferred them over French equivalents. Most American merchants had dealt only in a language and currency which they understood fluently.

Although the value of French purchases of American goods reached 9 million livres a year ($4.1 billion today), Americans never spent more than 2 million livres a year ($1.86 billion) on French products. France soon developed a trade deficit that combined with the huge cost for its part in the American Revolutionary War to collapse the French economy.

To add to France's collective distress, three years of drought had produced widespread famine and popular discontent when Jefferson arrived in 1787. With too little wheat in the fields to produce flour, prices of bread and other food staples had climbed 60% in a year, and food shortages left many families facing hunger and starvation.

The Paris assembly subsidized food purchases for the poor, but there was not enough money or bread to nourish everyone.

.

In Montmartre, north of Paris, 20,000 emaciated, unemployed peasants had migrated from the drought-stricken countryside to seek nonexistent manufacturing jobs they assumed the city could offer. They ended up sleeping in the streets and starving, with no prospects of even the most menial work—or a crumb of bread.

And in the eastern industrial suburb of Faubourg Saint-Antoine, hunger and despair gripped 50,000 unemployed workers and sent them into the streets rioting and looting.

"Paris is in danger of hourly insurrection for the want of bread," Jefferson concluded.

In the anterooms of the king's palace at Versailles, Lafayette and a group of noblemen developed a scheme that seemed to democratize power without doing so—much as Jefferson and the leaders of the American Revolution had done.

In writing America's Declaration of Independence, Jefferson had proclaimed "...all men...created equal"—even as more than 60,000 men, women, and children toiled across America as slaves and would continue to do so, with no rights to refuse. Jefferson himself owned more than 600 slaves and freed only one or two favorites (his own illegitimate sons) in his will.

As Jefferson looked on, the Marquis de Lafayette and a group of enlightened French noblemen voted to do much the same in France as the Americans. The result was a document entitled "The Declaration of the Rights of Man and the Citizen." Its adoption replaced almost

1,000 years of absolute monarchic rule with a quasi-constitutional monarchy—on paper, at least.

But the document fooled no one, adding not a crumb to the diets of starving French citizens.

In the country side, mobs attacked and burned the chateaux of rich noblemen, and in Paris, the desperate people of the Faubourg St. Antoine rose as one, storming down streets, smashing store windows—at first, to find food, then to vent their fury at authorities by besieging the hated fortress-like Bastille prison.

Although soldiers slaughtered the first attackers, the army suddenly broke ranks as its troops—almost all of them commoners—recognized fathers, brothers, and neighbors in the mob and turned against their nobleman officers. They spun their cannons about, and, as officers fled for their lives, aimed at the prison's walls.

On July14, 1789, they blasted a passage for the mob to enter and free the prisoners inside. To their disappointment, they found only seven, but discovered a huge supply of arms and ammunition that turned the mob into an armed force.

They climaxed their triumph by seizing the prison governor, dragging him to a lamppost, and, to the cheers of the mob of onlookers, hung him by the wrists and disemboweled him.

"Then it is a full-blown riot," the King asked when told of the violence.

"No, Sire," his aide replied. "It is a full-blown revolution."

Although Jefferson did not witness the fall of the Bastille and subsequent slaughter, radical friends he had made at one of the salon get-togethers took him to see the ruins of the prison

3. Hungry mobs stormed Bastille prison east of Paris on July 14, 1789, marking the start of a revolution that would end nearly 1,000 years of absolute monarchic rule in France.

the next day. He described the destruction as "an illumination of the human mind...which shall assure to them [the French] a good deal of liberty...."

As for the disembowelment of the prison governor, Jefferson responded calmly, saying, "The tree of liberty must be refreshed with the blood of patriots and tyrants. Rather than it [the French Revolution] should have failed, I would have seen half the earth desolated."[1]

He seemed to enjoy certain details of the rioting: "They [the mob] carried the governor and Lieutenant Governor to the Place de Grève, cut off their heads, and sent them through the city in triumph to the Palais Royale.... About the same instant, they seized...M. de Flesselles [equivalent to mayor of Paris] in the Hotel de Ville [City Hall]...and cut off his head."

Jefferson fell completely under the spell of the French Revolution—even describing king Louis XVI, who had provided the arms, ammunition, troops, and money to pay for American independence, as being "of weak mind and timid virtue." Ignoring

Louis's courage in warring against England to save America, he accused the king of being subject to his queen's whims.

His description of the queen was even more vicious: "Proud, disdainful of restraint, indignant at all obstacles to her will, eager in the pursuit of pleasure...her inordinate gambling and dissipations...called into action the reforming hand of the nation."

Even before the outbreak of the French Revolution, Jefferson had expressed his opposition to centralized executive power. When he learned the contents of the American Constitution, which had been enacted in his absence, he warned, "If some termination to the services of the chief magistrate be not fixed by the Constitution...his office...will in fact become for life and history shows how easily that degenerates into an inheritance.[2]"

Shortly thereafter, Jefferson sailed home to the United States to assume the post of Secretary of State under President George Washington in America's first elected federal government under the new constitution.

Jefferson's enthusiasm for the popular uprising in France, however, left French spy masters in the French Foreign Ministry devising a plot that would threaten American independence, cost Jefferson his job, and perhaps the heads of a French spy.

Chapter 2
A Detestable Project

Thousands roared their welcome as the fearsome 34-gun French frigate sailed into Charleston, South Carolina, harbor on April 8, 1793. Onlookers burst into a cacophonous chorus that echoed across the harbor:

*"Allons enfants de la patrie!"**

The lyrics [in English: "Arise, children of the fatherland!"] were those of *La Marseillaise*—the savage hymn of the 1789 French Revolution.

The mob at Charleston harbor was doing its best to serenade in his native tongue a colorfully dressed young Frenchman at the ship's bow doffing his feathered *chapeau*, and waving at the cheering throng.

A French Adjutant General, Edmond-Charles Genêt had sailed the Atlantic to the United States as first minister plenipotentiary, or ambassador, from the new French Republic to the United States of America.

The Kingdom of France had sent ambassadors to America before Genêt, but the execution of French king Louis XVI three months

*In English, "Arise, children of the fatherland," from *La Marseillaise*, words and music by Claude Joseph Rouget de Lisle, May, 1792. Also known as *Chant de Guerre pour l'Armée du Rhin*, or "War Hymn of the Army of the Rhine."

earlier in January had transformed the kingdom into a republic. So Ambassador Genêt—or, under the French Revolution's new rules of address,

4. French Adjutant General and Minister
Plenipotentiary Edmond Charles Genêt.

"Citizen Genêt"—had become the first ambassador between the world's first two modern republics.

What the welcoming crowd did not know, however, was that Citizen Genêt was also a master spy carrying two sets of instructions.

At the time, France was at war with Britain—the third time the two nations had warred with each other in the previous thirty years and the 41st time in the previous 1,000 years. One set of Genêt's instructions, which he announced publicly, directed him to establish warm diplomatic relations with the young American nation, while gently urging the American government to begin repaying in advance the loans France had made to support America's Revolutionary War.

"The French nation sets a high value upon the ties which unite them to the American people," Genêt's orders proclaimed, "ties which the [French] National Assembly has...shewn the desire to draw still closer.

The Executive Council prescribes to Citizen Genêt to exert himself to strengthen the Americans in the principles which led them to unite themselves to France; to make them perceive that they have no ally more natural or more disposed to treat them as brethren; that these sentiments are engraved in the hearts of all Frenchmen enlightened upon the true interests of their own country[3].

But Genêt carried a second set of instructions—secret instructions directing him to lure the U.S. into a commercial and political union with France and raise an army in America to help France recapture the territories France had lost to Britain and Spain in the Seven Years' War.

"Your mission requires of you very great activity," read the instructions, " but to be efficacious, this ought to be hidden."

That war—the first "world war" of sorts—had raged from 1756 to 1763. Austria, Saxony, Sweden, and Russia—each lusting for shares of the wealth that lay in the Americas—had joined France at war with Britain, Prussia, and Hanover. Hanoverian princes had acceded to the British throne in 1714 and sent mercenaries to support Britain in both the Seven Years War and, later, in the American War of Independence.

In the end, Britain and Spain, which joined the fray in the war's last year, stripped France of her huge North American empire—all of Canada, Louisiana, and the West Indies. In addition, Britain seized French colonies in Africa and India.

French kings Louis XV and his successor Louis XVI had hoped—in vain as it turned out—that French military and financial support of the American Revolution would weaken Britain enough to permit French re-conquest of Canada. Before she could do so, however, French revolutionaries at home overthrew the French monarchy.

As it turned out, the leaders of the French revolution—though commoners—were no less ambitious than their royal predecessors to amass colonial wealth, and they sent Genêt to recruit an American expeditionary force to help France do the job in North America.

By uniting the United States with France politically and militarily, French leaders hoped to reconquer Spanish Florida, Louisiana, and Canada and restore French control of what had been *La Nouvelle France.* With control of North America, the French would gain control of Atlantic sea lanes and leave Britain encircled, with her foreign trade and economy at the mercy of the French.

Genêt's immediate orders were to establish close personal ties to the self-proclaimed Francophile, Secretary of State Thomas Jefferson, and coax him into recruiting American fighting men for "the conquest of the two Floridas, Canada, and Nova Scotia."

As a United States envoy to France during the French Revolution, Jefferson had openly supported reducing the king's powers—even inviting leaders who opposed absolute monarchic rule to use his official residence in Paris as a meeting place.

Jefferson cheered French revolutionaries as they executed perceived enemies without trial and paraded their heads dripping blood on pikes through the streets of Paris.

Calling bloodshed a necessary by-product of revolution, Jefferson feigned some concern for justice, admitting, "Many guilty persons fell without trial, and with them some innocent.

> These I deplore as much as anybody...but I deplore them as I should have done had they fallen in battle.... The liberty of the whole earth was depending on the issue of the contest, and is ever such a prize won with so little innocent blood?... Rather than it [the French Revolution] should have failed, I would have seen half the earth desolated."[4]

His open support for the savage Paris slaughter stunned European leaders. In fact, only about two percent of the nearly 20,000 men, women, and children beheaded on guillotines during the French Revolution were members of the nobility or clergy, whom revolutionaries deemed responsible for food shortages that left France facing starvation.

The rest of the guillotine's victims were ordinary citizens—bakers and other shopkeepers, for example, charged without a crumb of evidence with hoarding flour and other essentials to raise prices.

French political leaders, now dominated by radicals, believed ambassador Jefferson's open support for the brutal political upheaval in France made him the perfect candidate as a double agent, or mole, ostensibly serving his native land while furthering the interests of his country's closest ally. He had after all reacted rather positively to the execution of king Louis XVI on the guillotine in January.

"I am not prepared to say that the first magistrate of a nation cannot commit treason against his country or is unamenable to its punishment," He expounded, then added: "I should have shut up the Queen in a convent...placed the king in his station, investing him with limited powers." But, he added, the "expunging" of the king had become a necessity in France given conditions there at the time.

—-

*Le jour de gloire est arrive.**

—-

The crowd on the Charleston waterfront seemed to agree as they roared the first of the savage words in the French national anthem when Genêt's ship tied up. They sang the same words—"the day of glory has arrived"—that hysterical

5. The execution of French king Louis XVI on the guillotine in the Place de la Révolution (now Place de la Concorde) in Paris in January 21, 1793.

*"The day of glory has arrived,"

mobs had shrieked on the *Place de la Revolution* [now *Place de la Concorde*] in Paris when the guillotine's knife sent the French king's head toppling into a blood-soaked basket.

American newspaper headlines that had hailed the king's execution now hailed Edmund Charles Genêt's arrival in America and urged Americans to respond to his call to resume their war against Britain.

"Every friend to the Rights of Man in America," wrote the editor of the *Boston Globe*, "will constantly feel an attachment for their French brethren. Let it be remembered that...[France] is contending the cause of Europe and America, and GOD grant her success."

In France, meanwhile, Gouverneur Morris, Jefferson's replacement as America's minister in Paris awaited his carriage after dinner as a mob marched by. Pushing and shoving each other, they dragged what appeared to be a living, albeit unrecognizable, human being, its clothes in tatters, blood pouring from every orifice, its face an unrecognizable mass of crushed flesh.

"This mutilated form of an old man of seventy-five," Morris reported, "is put to death and cut to pieces, the populace carrying about the mangled fragments with a savage joy. Gracious God, what a people!"[5]

After witnessing the gruesome reality of the French Revolution, Morris ignored protocol and, knowing Jefferson's bias in favor of French revolutionaries, he wrote to warn President Washington of the appointment of Edmond Charles Genêt as French ambassador to the United States. It arrived too late for Washington to prevent Genêt's appointment, however.

"I have seen Mr. Genêt and he has dined with me," Morris wrote. "He has, I think... the manner and look of an upstart...and may have rated himself a little too high. He chose America *as being the best harbor during the storm* [his italics], and...*he will not put to sea again until it is fair weather*, let what will happen"[6]

In a subsequent letter to Robert Morris [no relation], a close friend and confidante of the President, Gourverneur Morris enclosed documents listing what had been secret elements of Genêt's mission:.

"I am informed in a way that precludes doubt that the [French revolutionary] executive council has sent out by Mr. Genêt three hundred blank commissions for privateers to be given clandestinely to such persons he might find in America inclined to take them. They suppose that the avidity of some adventurers may lead them into...altercations with Great Britain and terminate finally in a war.... Waving all questions of honesty, it is in respect to us a detestable project."[7]

By disembarking in Charleston, Genêt had ignored—indeed scoffed at—normal diplomatic protocol and, in effect, threw down the gauntlet at the President of the United States.

Although infuriated by Genêt's conduct, Washington had no idea of Genêt's motives yet; Morris's letter had not revealed them, and Jefferson did nothing to clarify matters.

Indeed, Jefferson did everything he could to disguise the purpose of the Genêt mission.

"It is impossible for anything to be more affectionate, more magnanimous than the purport of his [Genêt's] mission," Jefferson all but purred as he tried soothing the President. Jefferson insisted that Genêt had pledged that France would do all in her power to promote peace and prosperity in America.[8]

—-

Contre nous de la tyrannie; l'étandard sanglant est levé[*]

—-

Without a spoken or written word, Genêt had nonetheless challenged the American President and every member of Congress. By commandeering a powerful 34-gun frigate to sail to America, he hoped to intimidate Americans—and their government—with a dazzling display of his country's military might as he landed in the New World.

In a show of disdain, he purposely skirted America's capital of Philadelphia and landed in Charleston, South Carolina, a hotbed of southern fury directed at the President and his government. In effect, he had thumbed his nose at diplomatic protocol and landed without immediately presenting his diplomatic credentials to the head of state. Genêt had good reason for insulting the President

The Revolutionary War had left the United States deeply in debt, and President Washington had proposed a tax every bit as high as—even higher than—the British taxes that triggered the Revolutionary War.

Indeed, Washington's proposed taxes had sparked a new call to arms in the South, and Genêt's arrival in Charleston on a warship seemed to promise southern protesters the same French military support for the overthrow of Washington's American government that

France had contributed to the overthrow of King George's British government.

—-

Entendez-vous dans les compagnes? Mugir ces féroces soldats![†]

—-

South Carolinians were particularly vicious in their opposition to Washington's new federal taxes, calling them unwarranted and unfair.

Although the Revolutionary War had left the federal government and many northern states mired in debt, southern states were relatively debt free and unwilling to pay for debts they had not incurred.

Nonetheless, three years before Genêt arrived in Charleston, U.S. Treasury Secretary Alexander Hamilton—a New York banker's son-in-law—had proposed that the federal government "fund" the nation's *total* Revolutionary War debts. His plan called for combining all state Revolutionary War debts with those of the federal government into a single capital fund, which the Treasury would cover by issuing and selling long-term, interest-bearing federal government bonds and collecting taxes to repay the borrowed money.

6. U.S. Secretary of Treasury Alexander Hamilton.

Hamilton's proposal drew hoots in Congress and rioting in parts of the South. Coming as it did after an eight-year war to end British efforts to tax them, the prospects of any American government tax shocked almost all Americans. Southern states such as South Carolina, however, were particularly outraged. South Carolina had repaid all its war debts and saw no reason to pay any debts incurred by northern states. South Carolina leaders argued, with some truth, that corruption and profiteering by public officials had inflated military costs in the North.

One reason southern state governments had avoided the huge debts of northern states was the social structure of the South, where wealthy oligarchs—mostly plantation owners—often recruited, paid, and led their own militiamen, while Northern state governments depended on state governments to recruit and fund state militias.

Before being named a general in the Continental Army, South Carolina Governor William Moultrie was an important planter. As commanding colonel of a state militia, he had recruited, outfitted, and armed his men out of his own pocket, then led them in combat, and prevented the British from landing in Charleston in 1776.

7. South Carolina Governor William Moultrie greeted Citizen
Genêt in his Revolutionary War general's uniform.

Having paid his troops what he owed them, Governor Moultrie was particularly angry—

indeed, infuriated—at the additional taxes he would owe to pay Continental Army troops because of congressional mismanagement.

In addition, Governor Moultrie and other Charlestonians had staked claims to and invested heavily in large tracts of unsettled western lands that the Washington Administration had promised to open and now refused to do so without added money in the U.S. Treasury.

Adding to the anger in Congress over funding of the long-term debt, Hamilton said the U.S. Treasury needed an immediate supply of funds for current expenses, which he proposed raising with a tax on whiskey. Such a tax, he said, would affect so broad a cross-section of the population that it would have only negligible effects on any single individual.

He badly miscalculated.

Farmers in western Pennsylvania alone owned about 5 percent of American whiskey stills; they converted surplus grains from every farmer in western Pennsylvania and neighboring states into whiskey. Indeed, whiskey had become fundamental to frontier economics in every state in Appalachia—Maryland, Virginia, North and South Carolina and Georgia. With no paper money available in most of the country, whiskey had become the currency of the West—much of it produced in home stills.

So proposals for taxes on whiskey had sent South Carolinians and Americans in the rest of the Appalachian states into paroxysms of fury by the time thirty-year-old Charles-Edmond Genêt sailed into Charleston harbor on April 8, 1793, and ordered his ship tied up at quayside.

—-

Ils viennent jusque dans vos bras![‡]

—-

"The crowd noise grew intolerable," Genêt said while grinning broadly and waving his hat at the throng to excite them even more. His eyes, however, constantly scanned scanning the front of the crowd looking in vain for a tall Virginian.

"We are pretty well assured of their good disposition," his instructions from the French secret service had predicted modestly

As he stepped off his ship, Genêt immediately added fuel to southern fury by mounting a platform and echoing words that the French chargé d'affaires had already proclaimed or published in towns across America:

Mes amis! Genêt cried out:

8. French ambassador Edmond-Charles Genêt arrived in America on the menacing 34-gun frigate *L'Embuscade* ("The Ambush").

"Men still live who can say, 'Here a ferocious Englishman slaughtered my father; there my wife tore her bleeding daughter from the hands of an unbridled Englishman.'

"Those same men can say, 'Here a brave Frenchman died fighting for American liberty; here French naval and military power humbled the might of Britain!'"

Although some in the crowd may have heard similar words before, his voice roused the huge supportive mob as never before. Indeed, they so roused Governor William Moultrie that he prepared to ask the state's assembly to reassert state sovereignty and independence.

And after the harbor-side celebration had ended, he promised Genêt, "The cause of France is our own."[9] South Carolina, he said, was ready to secede from the young American confederation and follow the mesmerizing Edmond Charles Genêt into union with France.

Chapter 3
A Spy Is Born

Edmond Charles Genêt was born on January 8, 1765, in the shadows of the great French royal palace at Versailles, 25 miles west of Paris.

Edmond's father, Edmé Genêt, was a commoner so brilliant he became a royal favorite and confidante of kings Louis XV and Louis XVI. His extraordinary talents quickly gained him access to almost every nook and cranny at the enormous Palace of Versailles—along with all the secrets they contained.

Two years before Edmé's son Edmond Charles was born, the end of the Seven Years' War had cost France her global empire and left the French government—and the King—all but bankrupt. The embittered French Foreign Minister Étienne François duc de Choiseul set the restoration of French hegemony in North America as his life's goal, and he turned to Edmé Genêt to help realize his goal.

As his first step, however, he needed the support of French king Louis XV.

"England is the declared enemy of your power," Choiseul warned Louis, "and she will be so always. Many ages must elapse before a durable peace can be established with this state [England], which looks forward to the supremacy of the four quarters of the globe."

9. French Foreign Minister Étienne François duc de Choiseul.

Ironically, Choiseul's description of Britain's global ambitions all but matched his own, as well as the King's, ambitions for France.

Choiseul saw his first opportunity to realize some of those ambitions when an avalanche of tax increases swept 40,000 Englishmen into debtor prisons and provoked anti-tax rioting by thousands of English farmers and workers

The Seven Years' War had left the victorious British government as bankrupt as the French, but as anti-tax rioting threatened to swell into a national rebellion, Parliament retreated, enacting sharp tax reductions to placate the angry mobs. It then hoped to compensate for lower revenues in Britain by imposing the first-ever direct taxes on Americans to pay for the military protection Britain provided to protect Americans against Native American raids.

To minimize the impact on the average consumer, Parliament simply extended the Stamp Act to Americans. In effect for decades in England, it required the purchase and affixment of one or more revenue stamps—often worth less than a penny each—on all legal documents (contracts, wills, deeds, marriage certificates, etc.), newspapers and periodicals, liquor containers, decks of playing cards and a host of other industrial and consumer goods.

Although negligible in its effects on the costs of a single item—a newspaper, for example—its cumulative returns to the government were enormous, because it required all taxpayers to purchase and attach a stamp on every document at each step along its path from producer to consumer—purchase orders at each transfer point, for example, and bills of lading along the multiple routes from producer to consumer.

With Americans scattered over so vast and sparsely settled a continent, London had expected little if any popular resistance to the tax.

London's intelligence proved more than faulty. Prominent leaders across America protested to London as never before—and they communicated their objections with each other—again, something the fiercely independent colonial leaders had seldom ever done.

"Our trade will be ruined," Boston's leading merchant-banker John Hancock complained.

Virginia planter George Washington was more blunt: "They have no right to put their hands in my pocket," he railed at Parliament.

When Parliament ignored their protests, angry colonists threatened to hang stamp agents and block the discharge of stamps from ships arriving from England. Worse, they launched colony-wide boycotts of British goods, all but ending commerce with England, in turn, threatening British merchants with mass bankruptcies and reducing British government tax revenues still further.. Now some of the British joined American protests against Parliament.

In Paris, Choiseul was ecstatic. The route to revenge against Britain seemed clear.

"England has discovered with surprise that her colonial possessions in America are the sources of much of the power which she enjoys,"

Choiseul crowed. "It is there that England finds the outlet for her manufactures."[10]

After Americans expanded their boycott of British goods across all thirteen colonies, British merchants felt the losses so deeply that they joined Americans in the protest *en masse*. Faced with massive election defeats, Parliament repealed the stamp tax a year to the day after it had enacted it—without having collected a penny of tax. Still more costly, Parliament had alienated several million of Britain's once-loyal colonists without reaping any benefits.

As once-loyal British subjects in America turned against their British overlords, Choiseul believed the way was clear for a French return to North America.

To implement his goal, he took command of the *Secret du Roi*, the super-secret—often deadly—intelligence office at the seat of government in the palace at Versailles. He then expanded its reach by folding into it the military and naval intelligence services, which sent agents in the guise of interpreters to every French embassy and consulate in foreign lands and to the side of every French diplomat or important French figure living or traveling overseas.

To direct intelligence operations, Choiseul promoted the forty-two-year-old Edmé Genêt, a renowned scholar and linguist with perfect credentials to head an intelligence service that disguised itself as a bureau of interpreters.

At the time, Genêt had a perfect command of most European languages. His knowledge of British politics, finance, and commerce—especially Anglo-American commerce—lured political and military leaders and merchant bankers to his door, seeking counsel. His Versailles *salon* became a center for marshals, cardinals, and ministers from all parts of Europe.

Two years later, when fifteen-year-old Marie-Antoinette arrived from Vienna to marry the king's grandson, Genêt made certain his talented oldest daughter became the future queen's closest friend and companion.

10. Fifteen-year-old Princess Marie Antoinette.

After Louis XV died, his inexperienced 20-year-old successor Louis XVI turned to the experienced diplomat Charles Gravier, Comte de Vergennes to take control of foreign affairs.

Vergennes lectured the young king: "The French king has the right to influence all the world's important matters. Her king is comparable to a supreme judge, entitled to regard his throne as a tribunal established by Providence.

> *England is the natural enemy of France....grasping, ambitious, unjust, and perfidious. The invariable, most cherished purpose of her policies has been ...the overthrow, humiliation and ruin of France.... All means to reduce the power and greatness of England...are just, legitimate, and even necessary, provided they are efficient. Placed in the center of Europe, France has the right to influence all great affairs... [France] must always be the first state in Europe.[11]*

With that he strode over to Edmé Genêt's office, dusted off plans to recapture North America, then marched into the new king's study with Edmé Genêt a step behind.

After studying hundreds of documents from French agents in England and America, including the secret proceedings of America's Continental Congress, Vergennes concluded:

11. French Foreign Minister

Charles Gravier Comte de Vergennes

"French agents have carefully outlined the course of the future Americans rebelling against England, including the identities of all participants and a description of the moment when the uprising in the American colonies would permit France to retake them...the entire scheme has been laid out, the paths cleared to success, with the names of colonist leaders ready to collaborate with France."[12]

At Vergennes's behest, Genêt ordered French agents in America to bribe colonial leaders to collaborate with France by offering "personal considerations" and pledging French financial and military help for a rebellion against British rule.

Within a year, the remaining thirteen American colonies would declare independence, and French government officials began planning a way to recover New France by embracing the American rebels and making them a part of a new French Union.

"Our primary interest," Vergennes reminded his head of intelligence, Edmé Genêt, "is to separate the English colonies from their mother country forever and prevent any kind of reunion between them. England is our first enemy".

Chapter 4

'A Glorious and

Happy Day'

At the very least, Genêt's spies assured him, and in turn, Vergennes, that a supply of French arms would allow the Americans to fight the British for years and leave the British military too weak to prevent French reconquest of her North American territories.

On March 20, 1778, Vergennes led Benjamin Franklin and two other U.S. envoys along the dazzling Hall of Mirrors in the Palace of Versailles to the Peace Drawing Room. At its south end, His Most Christian Majesty King Louis XVI awaited on an elevated gilded throne, resplendent in robes of snow-white ermine and flowing blue silk, appliquéd with gold fleurs-de-lis—the colors and symbols of the once glorious French empire.

Waving his golden scepter. Louis made a show of recognizing the new nation and agreed to send the Americans the military and financial assistance that Genêt and Vergennes had recommended.

Within a week, Vergennes appointed his close longtime aide Conrad Alexandre Gérard de Rayneval minister plenipotentiary [i.e., ambassador] to the United States.

A product of Genêt's school of intelligence, he received two sets of instructions—the usual public niceties in one set and a secret order in the second set "to watch carefully and warn Genêt if there were any indications the Americans might opt for reconciliation with England."

Vergennes and Genêt would now have a master of intelligence near the seat of government in America.

The Harvard-trained lawyer John Adams sensed the French government's motives behind the Rayneval mission:

> The Count de Vergennes instructed Mr. Conrad...to penetrate into the secrets of Congress and obtain from some of the members or some of the secretaries or clerks copies of the most confidential communications between Congress and their ministers.[13]

With none of its own ministers trained in espionage, Congress had had to rely on the blunt-talking Adams and the popular but doddering, seventy-year-old inventor Benjamin Franklin to serve as American emissaries in France. Compared to the soft-spoken Franklin, Adams made a terrible impression.

While the French hailed the philosopher-scientist Franklin as "the embodiment of the enlightenment, the crusty, 40-year-old John Adams was "quite out of his element" at the French court. "He cannot dance, drink, game, flatter, promise, dress, swear with gentlemen, and talk small talk or flirt with the ladies."[14]

12. John Adams was the first Founding Father to recognize nefarious motives for French aid in the American Revolution.

From the first, however, Adams recognized the nefarious motives of the French for supporting the American Revolution. "It has always been the...intention... of France," he maintained, "to encourage continuation of the war in America in hopes of exhausting [British] strength and resources...and depressing the rising power of America."[15]

In addition to their policies, the dandy mannerisms and laced shirt cuffs in French court repelled the earthy New Englander. He absolutely refused to wear court dress—or fawn at the feet of America's benefactors. Although he was grateful for French financial aid to America, he insisted that France had as much to gain from an American victory as the United States.

"Were it not for the United States," Adams argued, "England would be too powerful for the House of Bourbon."[16]

Adams's remarks so infuriated Vergennes that he refused to have further dealings with Adams and restricted his contacts on Franco-American matters to Franklin. All but ostracized by the French court, Adams found himself with little official business left to do and returned home with his son.

France later signed two treaties with the United States. One was a treaty of amity and commerce that gave each nation most-favored-nation status with the other.

A second treaty of alliance was to take effect only if and when war erupted between France and Britain. In that case, France pledged to "maintain effectually the liberty, sovereignty, and independence" of the U.S. The U.S. would have a free hand to conquer Canada and Bermuda, while France would have the right to seize the British West Indies. Each country guaranteed the other's territorial integrity and pledged not to conclude a truce or peace treaty with Britain without the other's consent.

The treaty took effect within weeks after a mid-June encounter between British and French naval forces.

Aware of imminent French engagement in the American land war, the British army withdrew from Philadelphia to consolidate northern forces on New York Island [Manhattan], which was more defensible than Philadelphia.

By July 4, Philadelphians had returned to their city to celebrate the anniversary of American independence. Congress resumed its deliberations on July 7, 1778, and five days later, the city erupted in joyful celebrations to welcome the French fleet and Conrad-Alexandre Gérard. Gérard was the first French ambassador—indeed the first foreign emissary from any nation—to the United States of America.

On May 2, 1780, 5,000 crack French troops under French General Jean Baptiste Donatien de Vimeur Comte de Rochambeau sailed from France with a strong naval escort.

By spring in 1781, George Washington had developed a scheme to combine his Continental Army with the 5,000-man French army and, with a powerful French navy, storm British defenses at Yorktown, Virginia. After a three-day siege the British had no choice but to surrender.

Yorktown proved to be the last great battle of the American War of Independence. Anglo-American peace talks began in Paris in the spring of 1782, and both sides agreed to peace in January 1783. On November 25, 1783, the last British troops sailed from New York, marking the beginning of the end of one great empire and the end of the beginning for another.

For France, however, American victory at Yorktown proved to be a two-edged sword. For a moment it seemed the partial fulfillment of Edmé Genêt's vision of crushing the historic French enemy Britain and recovering the great French empire in North America.

But then Edmé Genêt died.

Chapter 5
Like Father, Like Son

Edmé Genêt died in September 1781, a month before his vision of a French return to North America seemed about to become a reality with the decisive Franco-American victory at Yorktown, Virginia.

His death left France, her king, and Foreign Minister Comte de Vergennes without an administrator to head one of the French government's most important and complex functions.

Fortunately, Genêt had spared no effort training his successor, and Vergennes waited less than a day to invite him to assume Edmé Genêt's enormous powers:

"My friendship and esteem for your late father," Vergennes wrote to Edmé Genêt's son Edmond Charles Genêt, "have provoked a sincere concern, Sir, for you and your family and the grief you must be suffering. In my anxiety to relieve your distress, I am pleased to tell you, Sir, that the King has been gracious enough to offer you the office held by your late father. I hope that this evidence of the King's grace will serve as some consolation to you and your family."[17]

No man in France was better equipped to assume his father's role as French espionage chief Vergennes quickly recognized his brilliance by changing Genêt's title from clerk-in-chief to Assistant Secretary for Foreign Affairs, thus elevating him to cabinet rank as the second most important official in the Foreign Affairs Ministry.

Groomed from early childhood for the post, Genêt, more than any palace figure not of noble blood, had the king's confidence and devotion. He and the entire Genêt family were privy to the court's most guarded personal secrets. Genêt had entered his father's bureau as an apprentice translator at fifteen and won appointment the same year as personal aide to "Monsieur," as Louis XVI's next younger brother and next in line to the throne was called.

When Genêt turned sixteen, the King appointed him a lieutenant in the Corps of Dragoons. In the year that followed, Edmond Genêt learned English military and naval terms, studying with English prisoners of war before mustering out of the army and returning to Versailles.

In 1780, Vergennes took personal charge of the young man, then seventeen, He appeared more gifted even than his father in foreign languages, and he displayed startling—indeed, deceiving—good looks, exquisite taste in clothes, and a commanding military bearing and presence.

In 1781, after Genêt had completed a grand tour of Europe, Vergennes transferred Genêt to Vienna and the court of Queen Marie-Antoinette's family, but he returned to Versailles six months later when his father died. Not yet nineteen, young Genêt took the reins of the vast espionage network his father had commanded for thirty years. The son, like his father, seemed destined for an illustrious career.

One of young Genêt's first tasks was to carry the news of Yorktown to Vergennes and King Louis XVI. But after his first, exhilarating report to the king, he failed to keep participants under close enough surveillance, and the peace treaty they signed caught him, as well as Vergennes by surprise.

As the U.S., Britain, and France sat down to work out a peace settlement of the American war, U.S. Supreme Court Chief Justice John Jay, the third American peace negotiator with Franklin and John Adams, realized immediately that the French were purposely delaying consummation of a peace treaty between the United States and Britain.

"It is not in their interest," Jay believed. "They will therefore endeavor to plant such seeds of jealousy and perpetually keep our eyes fixed on France for security.... It is in their interest to keep some point or other in contest between us and Britain to keep us employed in the war and dependent on them for supplies."[18]

Convinced that the French government was intent on preventing peace and reducing America to an impotent French protectorate, Jay, Adams, and Franklin decided to disregard congressional instructions and violate the treaty of alliance with France.

On November 30, 1782, they surprised Vergennes by signing "provisional articles" of peace with England without French participation or knowledge. Jay and Adams especially had wanted to send a signal to France that the American states were now independent and would not submit to French interference in their foreign affairs.

To counter French efforts to capture American allegiance, British negotiators in Paris agreed to a peace settlement that gave the Americans all they had sought—and far more.

The men and boys who died in the Revolutionary War had fought for individual liberties, elimination of all British taxes, and relaxed parliamentary interference in colonial affairs. Few thought of independence when Americans staged their objections to the British Stamp Act in 1765.

Indeed, even the Suffolk Resolves in Massachusetts in 1774—a precursor to the Declaration of Independence—did not include a word about independence. It urged only that the people arm and defend themselves against British troops, halt all tax payments, and cease buying British goods. It also proclaimed:

> *That whereas his majesty, George the Third, is the rightful successor to the throne of Great-Britain, and justly entitled to the allegiance of the British realm, and agreeable to compact, of the English colonies in America—therefore, we, the heirs and successors of the first planters of this colony, do cheerfully acknowledge the said George the Third to be our rightful sovereign, and that said covenant is the tenure and claim on which are founded our allegiance and submission.*[19]

And at that late date, the Continental Congress representing all the colonies had agreed and had even approved and dispatched the so-called "Olive Branch Petition" to the British king seeking a peaceful solution to Anglo-American problems.

Signatories of the petition all pledged loyalty to the crown, but pleaded with George III to intervene to prevent Parliament from abridging the constitutional rights of British subjects in America.

It was not until the king brusquely rejected the petition that Americans felt they had little choice but to submit to British military rule or prepare for war.

In signing the provisional articles of peace after the revolution, Britain recognized American independence and ceded a vast territory that included the original thirteen colonies and all the lands stretching westward across the Great Lakes beyond Lake Superior and south along a line through the middle of the Mississippi River to the boundaries of Spanish Louisiana and Spanish Florida. Britain also granted the United States fishing rights off the Newfoundland and Nova Scotia coasts and navigation rights along the entire Mississippi River.

> *There shall be a firm and perpetual peace between his Britannic Majesty and the said States, and between the subjects of the one and the citizens of the other, wherefore all hostilities, both by sea and land, shall immediately cease. All prisoners, on both sides, shall be set at liberty; and His Britannic Majesty shall, with all convenient speed...withdraw all his armies, garrisons and fleets from the said United States, and from every port, place and harbor within the same.[20]*

In granting Americans all they had sought, England hoped to separate the United States from France and restore the rich commercial ties she had enjoyed with America before the war.

As a sign of good faith, the British evacuated Charleston, South Carolina, before the end of the year and reduced the strength of their New York garrisons.

Vergennes, however, was irate when he learned about the agreement. "I am at a loss, Sir, to explain your conduct and that of your colleagues towards us," he wrote to the self-proclaimed Francophile Franklin.

You have signed the preliminary articles without any communication between us despite your instructions from Congress forbidding any action without the participation of the King.... You are wise and sensible, Sir; you know the rules of decorum; you have done your duty all your life. Do you think you did so with respect to the King? I will not carry these thoughts any further, but will leave them to your own integrity.[21]

Recognizing that British concessions to the Americans "exceed all that I could have thought possible," Vergennes temporarily set aside his hopes for recovering *La Nouvelle France*.

On January 20, 1783, France signed preliminary articles of peace with Britain. Spain immediately followed suit. On February 4, Britain, France, and Spain proclaimed a cessation of hostilities. On April 15, Congress ratified the provisional articles of peace.

On November 25, the British evacuated New York Island, and as the last British troops left the docks, George Washington and New York Governor George Clinton, who had served as a brigadier general in Washington's Continental Army, rode into town together, with Clinton taking the reins of state government.

The loss of its trade monopoly in America, however, devastated the British economy and poisoned London's political atmosphere. But ironically, war's end was no less devastating for France, an ostensible victor.

Although France had avenged her military humiliation of the Seven Years' War and humbled her ancient British enemy, she had bankrupted herself without achieving the primary goal to recover the French empire in North America, to extend French influence across the rest of the continent, and to set French trade booming.

France paid a steep social as well as economic price for participating in America's revolution. Tens of thousands of French soldiers, sailors, and officials returned to France having witnessed for the first time individual liberties in a society that knew no royalty or nobility—and many liked what they saw.

"They imbibed a love of freedom nearly incompatible with royalty," according to Irish statesman-philosopher Edmund Burke, who served in the British House of Commons at the time.

"It seemed a grand stroke of policy to reduce the power and humble the pride of a great and haughty rival," Burke continued, "for as it was universally supposed that the loss of America would prove...a mortal wound to England, so it was equally expected that the power of the Gallic throne would increase thereby...and never again be shaken by any stroke of fortune."[22]

By fueling the flames of America's revolution, Vergennes and Genêt lit the funeral pyre of the Bourbon monarchy and the flames of the French Revolution. The French Revolution had a far different complexion than the American uprising. Indeed, the French conflagration would spark more than 200 years of revolutions, world wars, and state sponsored genocide across the globe.

Vergennes died in 1787 before he could see the effects of his political handiwork—or appoint a successor to Genêt to run the Bureau of Interpreters and its network of espionage agents.

His successor as foreign minister closed Genêt's bureau as part of a broad government spending cutback, exiling Genêt in St. Petersburg, where he languished for the next few years as French chargé d'affaires, attracting little notice in Paris from so distant a capital.

Back in France, however, Vergennes's policies had left the French economy in shambles, with farmers unable to grow enough to feed the French people. Even as he lay on his deathbed, politically ambitious rabble rousers were whipping up hungry French mobs into a frenzy of rioting, plunder, and slaughter that would plunge the nation into more than a decade of anarchy and genocide and Europe into continent-wide warfare.

Chapter 6
The Blood of
Patriots and Tyrants

Before the celebratory singing, dancing and drinking had ended when Britain released its hold on America, the newly independent United States of America found themselves as bankrupt as England and France.

Forced to pay for government services which Parliament had provided under British rule, America's state assemblies imposed or raised duties on goods imported from other states and foreign lands and then tried to do what the British could not: tax properties.

As they had under British rule, farmers and ordinary citizens across the country protested.

"What was it that caused the Revolution if it was not this?" an angry editorial writer in Philadelphia's *National Gazette* asked in support of protesters.

Jefferson called taxation "the most difficult function of government...against which citizens are most apt to be refractory."[23]

Farmers across the nation marched to state capitals, surrounding legislatures, demanding an end to taxes, forgiveness of debts, and return of all seized properties to former owners.

Farmers surrounded the state legislature in New Hampshire; Maryland farmers burned down the Charles County courthouse, and Virginia farmers burned down the King William and the New Kent county courthouses.

The 13 states had only just approved a constitution uniting them under a new government, and French agents now mixed with protesters, sowing seeds of dissent. "The French ambassador had instructions to block this enterprise," French foreign minister Charles-Maurice de Talleyrand-Périgord later disclosed.

> *This same ally that had sacrificed so much to separate the American states from England wanted to keep them disunited and separated from each other. [France] wanted to condemn them to a long and difficult infancy to keep them weak, without the means to govern or defend themselves effectively. The [French] ambassador obeyed his instructions...by opposing passage of the Constitution during the convention [in Philadelphia] and in each state legislature during the subsequent ratification proceedings. Although his efforts failed to block passage, they did help sow seeds of antifederalism that would sap United States strength.*[24]

In far off St. Petersburg, Russia, meanwhile, Charles Edmund Genêt—until then, a loyal servant of the French king—recognized the changes in the French political climate and concluded that his future—indeed, his life—might depend on demonstrating his allegiance to the new revolutionary government.

The revolutionaries who controlled the French National Assembly had outlawed the title "Monsieur" [literally, *"mon sieur,"* or "my sire"] and "Madame" [*"ma dame,"* or "my lady"] in favor of "Citoyen"—"Citizen"—and "Citoyenne" for women.

Genêt responded accordingly at a public audience of empress Catherine the Great, shocking and infuriating her by greeting her as *Citoyenne.*

As the Russian court and foreign diplomats gasped, she promptly ordered Genêt expelled from her presence, from the court, and, indeed, from Russia. She called him a *demagogue enragé*—an epithet hailed in the French press, which elevated Genêt to heroic levels among French revolutionary leaders.

Calling Genêt "a young man of ardent temper," American ambassador to France Gouverneur Morris wrote to President Washington in January 1793. Morris predicted that Genêt's rudeness to Catherine would "undoubtedly work in his favor" with the new French revolutionary government, given "the dearth of men" in government who embraced the Revolution as fervently as Genêt seemed to do.[25]

By the time Genêt returned to Paris, radicals had seized control of the French National Assembly, imprisoned the royal family and, on January 21, 1783 sent the king to his death before a huge crowd gathered around the guillotine on the Place de la Revolution, now the Place de la Concorde.

As Morris had predicted, French revolutionaries welcomed Genêt back to Paris as the only French diplomat "who had dared act like a free man" by confronting the Russian empress.[26] They promoted him to adjutant general in the army and agreed that his loyalty to revolutionary principles and his command of English made him the logical candidate as French envoy to the United States.

As famine continued undermining the national mood, Genêt convinced revolutionary leaders to reformulate the scheme devised by Vergennes and Genêt's father "to bind more and more the ties of friendship and fraternity [and] unite two free people," thus opening French access to America's agricultural plenty.

In February 1793, France sent its starving troops and untold numbers of hungry "volunteers" to overrun and plunder the fields and granaries of Belgium. Britain, Spain, Austria, Prussia and four other European monarchies responded by declaring war on France. Britain's fleet blockaded French ports and cut the flow of food and other essential supplies to France from the French West Indies and the United States.

Besieged on all sides and facing ever increasing famine, France called on her American ally to attack British and Spanish colonies in North America. The king of Spain responded by shutting the Mississippi River to all navigation by Americans. Americans in the West were ready to war against Spain to ensure that right and they turned to George Rogers Clark to organize a militia.

A hero in the American West, Clark had captured St. Louis and the Illinois country from the British during the Revolutionary War, but had subsequently fallen on hard times; deeply in debt, he had turned to drink.

Desperate to right himself and return to glory, Clark had written to the French government in the autumn of 1792 for financial and military support.

With Genêt's encouragement, leaders of the French Revolution decided to support Clark's venture and asked the United States government to do the same. Under the Franco-American treaty of 1778, France had sent troops, ships, and money to help Americans win independence from Britain. Now she called for repayment in kind.

"France," the Paris government assured the American government, "is not conducting a war against nations, but a defense of peoples against unjust aggression by kings."[27]

The French king's execution, however, had cost France far more of its former American friends than it had anticipated. Coming as it did after months of barbarity and bloodshed in the streets of Paris and other cities, the king's execution convinced President Washington that the French Revolution had little in common with America's War of Independence against Britain.

With France at war with both Britain and Spain, the President called his cabinet together to reassess foreign policy and determine whether America's 1778 treaty with France required engaging in a suicidal war with two powerful nations with whom America was ostensibly at peace.

The Franco-British war was already devastating the American economy. England had blockaded French ports and interrupted

Franco-American trade. Worse, the British were seizing untold numbers of American ships bound for France and impressing American seamen into British service.

Treasury Secretary Alexander Hamilton argued that rather than war with Britain, the United States should seek a trade agreement that would end the depredations.

A towering hero in the American Revolution and a close aide to Washington, Hamilton had the President's ear. A lawyer by profession, Hamilton pointed out that the 1778 Franco-American treaty was a defensive alliance, whose military obligations applied only when a third nation attacked one of the signatories.

"France being on the offensive in the present war," Hamilton pointed out, "our guarantee cannot take place and the United States ought to refuse a performance of that guarantee if demanded."[28]

In addition to his strict reading of treaty terms, Hamilton argued that the United States had signed the treaty with king Louis XVI, not with the revolutionaries who had killed the king.

Under the "laws of nature" at the time, the king *was* the state—*l'état c'est moi*—and the French royal family in exile had already proclaimed Louis's son the new king of France. Hamilton urged Washington to ignore the treaty until the new king mounted the throne. He urged the President not to receive a new ambassador from France until then.

Secretary of State Jefferson all but howled in disagreement. He did not like Hamilton, considered him a royalist. He argued that nations make treaties, not governments, and they remain in force regardless of changes in government. Failure to observe the 1778 Franco-American treaty, he insisted, would undermine the nation's honor and "gratify the combination of kings with the spectacle of the only two republics on earth destroying each other."[29]

He charged Hamilton with favoring "the confederacy of princes against human liberty...under pretense of avoiding war.[30]

Calling France America's "true mother country...since she has assured to them their liberty and independence," Jefferson ignored the ruthless slaughter taking place in France and insisted that "the liberty of the whole earth depends on the success of the French Revolution."[31]

Washington's trusted secretary Tobias Lear presented the President with a different point of view:

> *The universal hope is that they [the United States] may not be drawn into it... Some there are who deprecate the whole French nation—and who would be highly gratified in being able to impress their own sentiments upon the people at large in this country.*
>
> *On the other hand, some are as enthusiastically disposed in favor of everything that relates to the French and consider this Country as under an obligation to give the most unequivocal proof of its attachment to and preference of that nation.*
>
> *These two parties, however, are not thought to comprehend a very large part of the people; the general and commanding sentiment seem to point to a cautious and prudent line of conduct"[32]*

In the absence of constitutional guidance, the President took Lear's advice to heart and searched for a middle course that incorporated the best elements of the Hamilton and Jefferson arguments.

To favor either the British or the French, he knew, could trigger a shot that would plunge the United States into a global war and probably cost the young nation its independence. He could not—would not—take that chance. He decided on a different, albeit dangerous course.

Chapter 7
The Most Dangerous Mischief

As the crowd roared its approval, Charleston joined Governor Moultrie in adopting Genêt's cause as its own. Governor Moultrie ignored the federal Constitution by helping Genêt commission four privateers, which set out to sea to attack British shipping off the American coast. The promise of plunder lured hundreds of hungry, unemployed American seamen to sign on to Genêt's ships.

In the ensuing months they captured dozens of British vessels for French consuls to sell or refit with cannons to expand Genêt's fleet. To Charleston's delight, Genêt was doing what Washington had refused to do: join America's former Revolutionary War ally and wage war on Britain.

"Of the vessels armed at Charleston," Jefferson reported, "he [Genêt] said that on his arrival there he was surrounded suddenly by Frenchmen full of zeal for their country, pressing for authority to arm with their own means for its assistance, that they would fit out their own vessels, provide everything, man them and only ask a commission from him; that he asked the opinion of Governor Moultrie on the subject, who said he knew no law to the contrary but begged that whatever was to be done might be done without consulting him, that he must know nothing of it &c. Genêt thereupon gave commissions to the vessels; he was of the opinion he was justified not only by the opinions at Charleston but by our treaties."[33]

Building on his base in Charleston, Genêt organized a network of agents to encourage American support for a French war to recover control of Canada, Louisiana and the rest of the North American empire that France had lost to England and Spain at the end of the Seven Years' War in 1763.[34]

Within weeks after Genêt's arrival, French agents had organized American dissidents into nearly 40 "Democratic Societies" across the United States, merging some into "Democratic Clubs" that Jefferson's supporters had originally formed to help him chase his presidential ambitions.

In Georgia, frontier farmers had already overrun territory the United States had ceded to the Creek Indians and called for secession from the U.S. and establishment of either an independent state or a French protectorate.

With 250 blank military and naval commissions for qualified officers to lead the assaults, Genêt promised Indian fighter Elijah Clarke $10,000 cash and a commission as a French major general to lead two divisions of Carolinians and Georgians into Spanish Florida.

In Clarke, Genêt found a fervent Jacobin to recruit Southern frontiersmen who had suffered more than a decade of savage Indian and Spanish raids went "recruiting-mad for the French service."[35]

Genêt dubbed Clark's command the "Legion of Revolution and Independence of the Mississippi." Its orders were to "free" the Mississippi valley and New Orleans from Spain.

Clark, of course, had led the western campaign of the Revolutionary War in Illinois, Ohio, Indiana and Kentucky. He now took advantage of growing secessionist sentiment by recruiting more than 2,000 Kentuckians with promises of 1,000-acre land grants each in any Spanish territory they conquered. More than 4,000 Kentuckians signed "intents" to enlist if and when the fighting began.

Clark assured Genêt that once he received commissions for his officers and money for boats, guns and ammunition, his army would be ready to seize control of the Mississippi River Valley and form a new, French satellite nation incorporating all the lands west of the Appalachians.

Still working out of Charleston, Genêt sent French agents to New Orleans to incite insurrection by French Creoles who had chafed under

Spanish rule after France had ceded the area in the 1763 Seven Years' War settlement.

Since then, the Creoles had appealed regularly for French government help in overthrowing Spanish rule. Genêt now promised to give it to them.

In Philadelphia, Secretary of State Thomas Jefferson concealed Genêt's activities from the President.

Jefferson's silence did not result from ignorance. The new American minister in Paris, Gouverneur Morris, had warned that Genêt's political party had launched a propaganda campaign in Europe and announced his intention to "erect the standard of liberty everywhere."

Jefferson admitted to his son-in-law that the French regime had been "guilty of great errors in their conduct towards other nations, not only uselessly insulting crowned heads but endeavoring to force liberty on their [royalist] neighbors.[36] Nothing about Genêt's conduct, therefore, surprised Jefferson. Indeed, he encouraged it

Treasury Secretary Hamilton was incensed, however, calling Genêt's actions "an affront and injury of a very serious kind" and warning the President, "It is manifestly contrary to the duty of a Neutral Nation to suffer itself to be made an *instrument* of hostility by one power at war against another. In doing it, such a Nation becomes an Associated Party and risked becoming an accomplice in the hostility."

Hamilton went on to rail at Genêt's activities:

> *The manning and commissioning of vessels of war, the enlisting, levying or raising men for military service, whether by land or sea...are among the highest and most important exercises of sovereignty. They who undertake to enlist soldiers in a foreign country without the sovereign's permission and whoever alienates the subjects of another violates one of the*

most sacred rights both of the prince and the state. Foreign recruiters are hanged immediately and very justly.... It is manifestly contrary to the duty of a Neutral Nation to suffer itself to be made an instrument of hostility by one power at war with another. In doing it, such a nation becomes an associate.[37]

By April 18, 1793, a mere ten days after his arrival in America, Genêt's plans were complete:

"I have prepared the revolution of New Orleans and Canada," he boasted in a letter to the French foreign minister in Paris. "I have destroyed the maritime commerce of the English in these waters."[38] He said he needed only to rally the American people to force President Washington to support him with additional troops, weapons, and funds—or resign in favor of the Francophile Jefferson.

By then, Genêt envisioned toppling the recalcitrant Washington and seating Jefferson in Washington's place. Jefferson raised no objections.

With his privateers marauding British ships along the coast, Genêt left what had become his headquarters in Charleston for the first time since arriving in America. He set out for the nation's capital Philadelphia in a coach-and-four on what metamorphosed into a triumphal procession. Warned of his approach, Jefferson's Democratic Clubs in each town hailed Genêt's approach as a Second Coming.

Governor Moultrie added to the hysteria by sending messengers ahead "to announce me to the people" along the route and personally escorted him to Camden, South Carolina, where the heroic Baron de Kalb had fallen in the American Revolution. Genêt's own agents also preceded him from town to town to herald his coming and assure tumultuous welcomes with barrels of free rum and whiskey.

Church bells tolled his approach, cannons boomed, French flags flapped in the wind, and thirsty crowds slathered the free-flowing liquor, belching "hip-hip-hoorahs" for France with each swallow. In many communities, town fathers took up (and—as often as not—pocketed) collections to buy food for starving Frenchmen.

His journey grew into what he called "a succession of civic festivals." In almost every town, he said he found himself "clasped in the arms of a multitude that rushed out to meet me" to express "the fraternal sentiments of the American people for the French people."[39] At each stop, he expected to see Jefferson appear to help incite the crowds even more, but. Jefferson never showed.

Wherever possible, Genêt fed his agents enough funds to organize new 'Democratic Societies" to inflame passions for war with Britain and promote Franco-American ties. Many coalesced with supporters of Jefferson to succeed Washington as president, who was considering retiring at the end of his first term the following March, 1794.

Genêt's agents, meanwhile, remodeled the "Democratic Societies" after the Jacobin clubs in France. Organized by local radicals, each club collected dues to pay its expenses and build a firm, popular domestic base to do the organizer's political bidding.

Used extensively by Nazis and Communists in the 20th century, such clubs proved an effective, inexpensive, and relatively bloodless method of foreign conquest as club members gradually won or seized control of local governments.

Instead of draining national treasuries for armies to battle for every inch of foreign territory, a handful of local agents simply organized and prompted the disaffected in individual communities to rebel and overthrow their own local governments—sometime by "free" staged elections; sometimes by force.

After raising the banner of international brotherhood, the newly empowered local officials would welcome French occupying authorities and join other communities in converting their nation into a French puppet state.

Before Genêt left Charleston, he had not only organized a "Democratic Club" there, he had "honored" its members by enrolling them as honorary members of the original Paris Jacobin Club that had ignited the French Revolution.

By the time Genêt reached Richmond, Virginia, news of his activities had plunged the national capital of Philadelphia into crisis and widened the already bitter divisions in Washington's cabinet and in Congress

Washington was irate, fearing that Genêt's activities would provoke Britain into declaring war on the United States.

As usual, Jefferson tried calming the President, arguing that if Genêt's military schemes succeeded they might extend United States sovereignty over Spanish Florida, while a French flag over Louisiana would restore American navigation rights on the Mississippi River—rights that the Spanish had steadfastly refused to renew.

. Hamilton railed at Jefferson and pressed the President to issue a proclamation of neutrality.

Seeking to build circulation and revenues, the press added to the acrimony. The Jeffersonian *New York Journal* claimed the nation's honor depended on Washington's adherence to the 1778 treaty with France, with an immediate declaration of war against America's former oppressor, Britain.

The Hamiltonian press thundered its reply: "The friendship of France, instead of being a blessing, is to be dreaded by the United States as the most dangerous mischief. Her *enmity* alone can save us from ruin.... The French government professes to be pursuing liberty while it is extending its territories."[40]

Washington continued searching for a middle ground to keep the nation out of war, but in the end, did nothing. Indeed, his every word seemed to provoke more arguments among his cabinet members as they tried to work out a solution for what was still a new form of government without precedents in world history.

They had but the Constitution as their guide, but as magnificent as it was in principle, it remained frustratingly vague, without specific guidance for resolving practical questions of the men who had to govern.

Jefferson pointed out that the word *neutrality* did not appear in the Constitution. But because neutrality was "a declaration that there should be no war," it fell within the purview of Congress, not the President. Congress alone, he insisted, had the prerogative of declaring or not declaring war.

But Washington had begun to side with his treasury secretary and think that he should dismiss his secretary of state.

In the end, however, the President ignored both men and even the Constitution by issuing his own, original, formal proclamation, which he called "substantial" and, in effect, gave it the force of law [see Appendix].

On April 22, while careful to keep his options open by avoiding the word "neutrality," he declared the United States *at peace* with both Britain, France and all other combatants and said the nation would engage in "conduct friendly and impartial toward all the belligerent powers."

Washington set a precedent that every administration would follow for two centuries thereafter—namely, that treaties bound nations together regardless of changes in governments. So he left the 1778 treaties with France in place, but agreed with Hamilton that France had engaged in an offensive, not defensive, war, and that the earlier treaties did not apply to the current conflict.

To avoid entangling the nation in war, Washington warned Americans that "to involve ourselves in the contests of European nations...[is] unwise in the extreme" and would "put the nation's fragile economy and very existence at risk."

In the end, Washington had worked out a compromise that avoided the word *neutrality*, while forbidding Americans "to take part in any hostilities on the seas" or carrying "any of those articles deemed contraband by the modern usage of nations."

It also enjoined Americans "from all acts and proceedings inconsistent with the duties of a friendly nation toward those at war."[41]

In a direct response to Genêt's activities in Charleston, he banned the outfitting of privateers by foreigners on American territory.[42]

The proclamation was one of the most important acts of Washington's presidency, raising what he expected to be another pillar of presidential power—in effect, reinforcing his powers over foreign policy, national defense, and finance. In the end, he had invented—usurped?—a new presidential power: a power to issue proclamations with the force of law.

The Constitution, of course, gave the President no power to issue any proclamation of war, peace, neutrality, or anything else, for that matter, despite Hamilton's assertions to the contrary. In doing so, Washington again assumed a power that the Constitution had specifically reserved to the legislature.

Americans were quick to react. Freed from British ties for only a decade, most remained bitterly divided in their allegiances, with many retaining deep emotional and familial connections to their former motherland and longing to return to Britain's embrace.

Most others, however, harbored smoldering hatreds that flared up in riotous street demonstrations. Apart from the American-born, some 50,000 Irish immigrants needed not so much as a thimble of rum to spill out of taverns and rail against British persecution in Ireland—or assault passersby whose clothes were a cut too English.

Adding to the anti-British fervor were 30,000 Frenchmen—a mix of former officers and soldiers from the American Revolution and refugees from Acadia, Canada, whom the British had brutally ripped from their homes and shipped starving and penniless to alien shores for refusing to swear allegiance to Britain.

Newspaper editors—concerned with increasing their circulation and resulting profits—did everything they could to incite both sides. They appealed to Anglophiles—charging the French with "contending for plunder and empire"–and to Francophiles, charging the British with inciting Native American raids against settlers in the West and failing to evacuate western frontier posts.

They raged at the British, as well, for impressing American sailors into the British navy. Some charged Britain with planning to send invading armies to reclaim their former American colonies.

Washington, meanwhile, had no way to enforce his proclamation—no federal police force, as such, to ensure public observance of any federal laws.

He called on state governors to enforce his proclamation, but all he could do himself was order Treasury Secretary Hamilton to alert the Treasury's 500 customs agents and tax collectors to watch for contraband shipments destined for belligerent nations.

With no navy to enforce Washington's order on the high seas, antifederalist governors intent on weakening presidential powers reasserted claims of state sovereignty that Jefferson espoused.

"I believe," Jefferson stated, "that individual states have the right and power to reject as "null and void" any federal legislation they deemed an exercise of undelegated constitutional authority." In effect, Jefferson declared the President's proclamation null and void.

With Jefferson's apparent support, states with functioning harbors opened them to let Genêt's ships sail in and out with captured British cargo vessels.

The ships he captured, in turn, lured hundreds of unemployed ship fitters back to work to refit them as warships.

Genêt soon had a fleet of more than eighty armed vessels to patrol American coastal waters and capture British ships and cargoes. In addition, he and French consuls in major cities recruited a 1,600-man army of American volunteers who awaited Genêt's command to invade

Florida and seize it from Spanish control. In effect, Genêt had built a small empire within an empire.

Although a few newspapers praised the president's wisdom for following the path of neutrality, most still called for war on one side or the other—again, to sell newspapers.

Pro-British newspapers condemned the savagery, anarchy, and godlessness of French revolutionaries and warned Americans against propaganda that France was fighting for liberty.

"The French," wrote New York editor Noah Webster, "are contending for plunder and empire."[43]

The pro-French press displayed equal wrath against the British for refusing to evacuate troops from America's western frontiers in accordance with the 1783 peace treaty. They charged the British government with planning to try to reclaim their former colonies.

Adding fuel to the press war, Genêt sought to taunt the president by exposing presidential impotence.

He bought boldfaced newspaper advertisements calling on American "Friends of France" to ignore Washington's Neutrality Proclamation and enlist in the French service to fight the British.

"Does not patriotism call upon us to assist France?" his advertisements asked. "As Sons of Freedom, would it not become our character to lend some assistance to a nation combating to secure their liberty?"[44]

Jefferson constantly defended Genêt, while Hamilton, Knox, and Randolph all sided with the President, calling Genêt's actions in arming privateers in American waters "an affront to American sovereignty."

Genêt's fleet of privateers, however, rendered the debate over neutrality all but moot, as they sailed in and out of American harbors with impunity. In a direct challenge to presidential authority, Genêt's frigate *l'Embuscade*—the same ship that had carried him from France to Charleston—sailed into the nation's capital of Philadelphia on May 2, its guns in full view towing a British ship it had captured in American waters of Delaware Bay. The French ship flew the British flag upside down beneath a French flag.

British ambassador George Hammond was irate and threatened war with the United States for violating Washington's neutrality pledge.

Attorney General Edmond Randolph, the former Virginia governor, agreed the seizure by the French was illegal, and, on Washington's orders, Secretary of State Thomas Jefferson stepped out of character by demanding that the French return the English vessel to the owners. Two days later the French complied, without a word of protest from Genêt.

"It has been an extremely fortunate circumstance," Hammond wrote to British foreign secretary Lord Grenville, "that almost immediately after the appearance of this declaration of neutrality, events should have arisen that brought the sincerity of it to a practical test."[45]

In effect, Washington's Neutrality Proclamation established a new principle of international law as well as American constitutional law–namely, the concept of neutrality and the rights of nonparticipating neutral nations in wartime *not* to go to war.

Although rules abounded governing relations between warring nations, the world had ignored the rights of neutrals until George Washington raised the issue. [A year later, he would issue the American Neutrality Code of 1794.[46]].

Genêt approached Philadelphia convinced by his successive overland receptions that "the ardent and sublime love of the good country people...for the principles of France" had spawned "a very distinct party" in opposition to President Washington and neutrality. Aside from Genêt's mesmerizing voice, the free-flowing rum and beer that Genêt's advance men poured for all comers helped inflate their numbers considerably.

When he reached Philadelphia on May 16, *l'Embuscade* awaited in the harbor, its forty-four guns primed to fire into the air to signal Genêt's arrival.

As the first blast sounded, Philadelphia's church bells begin pealing; thousands of Philadelphians rushed into the streets to cheer and march—and discard all pretenses of neutrality or loyalty to their president.

"The bosoms of many hundreds of freemen beat high with affectionate transport," Genêt exulted, "their souls caught in the celestial fire of struggling liberty."[47]

An estimated 5,000 supporters rallied outside Genêt's hotel window and "sent their attachments" to France echoing across the city. One hundred of Philadelphia's leading citizens feted Genêt with an "elegant civic repast" that evening at Philadelphia's largest banquet hall.

Pennsylvania Governor Thomas Mifflin was first to toast the French envoy. A former merchant who had profited by hoarding food supplies and creating food shortages at Valley Forge during the bitter winter of 1778, Mifflin had resigned from Washington's military staff in disgrace.

Now he stood unabashed as he toasted the French envoy bent on asserting French control over the United States.:

"The Republics of France and America," he called out as he raised his glass, "May they be forever united in the cause of liberty.... May the United States of America, in alliance [with France] declare war against England."[48]

As the flags of France and the United States fluttered atop the hotel, guests—many of them state and federal officials—intoned fifteen more toasts' The last culminated in a chorus of cheers as Genêt donned the cockaded red liberty cap of the French Revolution and led the audience in singing "God Save the Rights of Man," to the melody of *God Save the King:*

God save the rights of man!
Give us a heart to scan
Blessings so dear:
Let them be spread around
Wherever man is found,
And with the welcome sound
Let us with France agree
And let the world be free...

The embarrassingly puerile lyrics lasted through four stanzas, followed by a cacophonous chorus of *La Marseillaise*.

Complementing the chorus of Philadelphia's drunken political leaders was the noisy arrival of the French fleet from the Antilles. Genêt went out to greet it, then ordered gangways lowered and sent the French seamen to join the Jacobin mobs in the crowded streets.

"The town is one continuous scene of riot," the British consul wrote in panic to his foreign minister in London. "The French seamen range the streets by night and by day, armed with cutlasses and commit the most daring outrages. Genêt seems ready to raise the tricolor and proclaim himself proconsul. President Washington is unable to enforce any measures in opposition."[49]

Drunken French sailors inevitably joined pro-French Americans on street corners demanding Washington's head, and Genêt responded by sending the President an ultimatum "in the name of France" to call Congress into special session and let that body choose between neutrality and war.

Genêt warned Washington that if he refused to let Congress declare war against Britain, he, Genêt, would "appeal to the people...the decisions of the President....

"I have acquired the esteem and the good wishes of all republican Americans by tightening the bonds of fraternity between them and ourselves," Genêt ranted. He predicted that Americans would "rally from all sides" to support him and "demonstrate with cries of joy...that the democrats of America realize perfectly that their future is ultimately bound with France."[50]

Washington's presidential edifice was tottering. With no law enforcement arm at his disposal, his pillars of power seemed hollow and ready to collapse, along with the new American republic.

Chapter 8
"We Ought To Form
One People"

Demonstrations raged night after night, into each successive day, growing more tumultuous as evening darkness enveloped the town.

Vice President John Adams described "the terrorism excited by Genêt in 1793, when 10,000 people in the streets of Philadelphia, day after day, threatened to drag Washington out of his house and effect a revolution in the government or compel it to declare war in favor of the French Revolution and against England."

Adams said Washington's residence had been "surrounded by an innumerable multitude from day to day, buzzing, demanding war against England, cursing Washington, and crying success to the French patriots and various Republicans."

Adams said he "judged it prudent and necessary to order chests of arms from the war office" to protect his own house.[51]

Washington feared for the safety of his wife and the flock of small children in his and her care. He considered sending them all to the safety of Mount Vernon.

Only Treasury Secretary Alexander Hamilton perceived the dangers to the nation of the Genêt-Jefferson collaboration, pointing out that the men who had organized Genêt's reception in Philadelphia "were the same men who have been uniformly the enemies and the disturbers of the government of the United States."[52]

Hamilton's warnings against Genêt frightened Jefferson. Rather than engage in a public feud with Hamilton that might reveal his own ties to Genêt, the Secretary of State turned to his friend and political ally Congressman James Madison.

"Nobody answers him [Hamilton]," Jefferson wrote to Madison, carefully omitting his motive. "For God's sake, my dear Sir, take up your pen, select the most striking heresies, and cut him to pieces in the face of the public. There is nobody else who can and will enter the lists with him."[53]

Madison wanted no part of Jefferson's feud with Hamilton, however—or his ties to Genêt. Although he did his mentor's bidding and wrote five articles critical of Hamilton, they were bland, and Hamilton responded with far more fire.

Signing nine essays in the *American Daily Advertiser* as "No Jacobin," Hamilton blistered Genêt:

"It is publicly rumored in this city," Hamilton charged, "that the minister of the French republic *has threatened to appeal from the President of the United States to the people.*"

Hamilton assailed Jefferson for supporting Genêt. Although he omitted Jefferson's name, he nonetheless skewered his fellow cabinet member: "What baseness, what prostitution in a citizen of this country to become the advocate of a pretension so pernicious, so unheard of, so detestable."[54]

In a cabinet meeting that followed, Hamilton repeated charges by European leaders that Genêt sought to export the French Revolution to America. He demanded that Jefferson display all his notes from meetings with Genêt and any notes pertaining to the "Democratic Clubs." Jefferson mounted a weak defense, saying any revelations about the democratic societies would interfere with the constitutional right of assembly.

By then, however, Washington had grown weary of Jefferson's obsessive defense of Genêt and left the cabinet room to consider Hamilton's arguments.

Genêt meanwhile made a show of trying to calm the Washington administration, reassuring Jefferson of France's deep love and respect for the United States. He told Jefferson he had no intention of luring

America into a war she could not afford. He said he hoped Americans would join France in cherishing peace and prosperity.

"Our republic, founded like yours... on equality, ought to be yours truly...we ought in some sort to form one people."[55]

He then tried enlisting Jefferson in the local Philadelphia Democratic (read Jacobin) Club, promising its support for his election to the presidency at the appropriate time. Although Jefferson made a show of reluctance about joining an organization openly critical of the government he served, he could not resist supporting Genêt, assuring his fellow Virginian, Congressman James Madison, that Genêt "offers everything and asks nothing."

Like Jefferson's other remarks about Genêt, his letter to Madison remains evidence of either profound naiveté or a determination to change the structure of the government of the United States.

Meanwhile, Genêt pounced like a hungry jungle cat to stir further disorder—as his instructions had urged:

> *In order to make your representations more effective, [you are] to direct opinion by means of anonymous publications. The Boston and Baltimore gazettes will be the best ones to use...to turn aside suspicion of authorship from you; but the more you contrive to influence public opinion, the more...[it] must be kept secret so as not raise alarm.... Your mission requires of you a great deal of astute activity, but to be effective, it must be secret.[56]*

Accordingly, Genêt spewed anti-British venom in pseudonymously signed articles and letters to the press in major towns across America. All closed with assurances that France "repels every idea of aggrandizement" and wants only "to assist" oppressed people in ridding their lands of despots.[57] Newspapers across America reprinted his articles.

"Minds were electrified," he chortled. "All the gazettes of the continent were filled with articles, each stronger than the others in favor of our cause." One gazette, he laughed, printed a cartoon depicting Washington's head dropping into a waiting basket by the stroke of the guillotine blade.[58]

Noah Webster's *New York Spectator* tried countering Genêt's propaganda with stern warnings:

> "The French government professes to be pursuing liberty while it is extending its territories.... It pretends great friendship for nations which it intends to conquer. In the face of friendly declarations...the French government has annexed the little, helpless republic of Geneva. Holland is enslaved...its money gone, its trade ruined. Venice has been annihilated—divided and sold. So much for the promised respect which France was to pay to the independence of other nations."[59]

Despite Webster's attack, Genêt's propaganda quickly gained traction in Philadelphia, where his network of agents filled the air in taverns and on street corners with anti-British rhetoric—stirring hatred everywhere, encouraging depredations against suspected Tories and their properties.

Under his name, letters went out to French agents across the United States, spinning a vast, intricate web of affiliated groups which Genêt could use to influence popular thinking and government policies.

A word from Genêt unleashed a flood of letters to the press praising France, denouncing England, and, often, assailing Washington and neutrality. A snap of his fingers sent orators to street corners to rally "all good republican citizens to arm themselves...with such implements of war as may be necessary for their defense."[60]

Across the nation, Genêt's agents grew more aggressive, openly calling for overthrow of Washington, attacking the taxes he had imposed. Others took a different tack, saying, "He who is an enemy of the French Revolution ought not to be entrusted with the guidance of any part of the machine of government."

A club member in Virginia called out, "Let us unite with France and stand or fall together."[61] And in Philadelphia, Genêt decided to reveal hitherto secret details of his mission in a letter to his political dupe Jefferson. It read, in part:

> "All obstacles raised by enemies of liberty having been removed, the French Republic, recognizing Americans as our brothers, has decreed all its seaports open to American ships, with all their rights and benefits therein extended to them. Moreover, the French Government has charged me with proposing to your government a liberal family pact uniting the two peoples commercially and politically."[62]

Genêt went on to propose mutual naturalization of the French and American people, mutual nationalization of industry and trade, mutual defense of each other's national interests, with French warships based in American ports to prevent ships of enemy nations such as Britain *from entering.*

The proposal shocked Washington; he ordered Jefferson to issue an immediate reply to Genêt that only the Senate could consider treaties and that it was in recess until late fall.

Washington's order to Jefferson was a spur-of-the-moment diplomatic fiction aimed at slowing the pace of Genêt's frightening campaign to enlist Americans in the imposition of French control over North America.

With Washington apparently helpless to control the spread of Genêt's malignant propaganda campaign, Genêt decided to confront the president directly, not just as French envoy, but as de facto leader of a powerful political force in America and a sizable fleet of ships in American ports and offshore.

His privateers were decimating British offshore shipping, while a French government fleet sat ready to sail from the West Indies to attack Nova Scotia. And armed bands of American recruits stood poised about the United States ready to seize control of several western states and invade Canada, Florida, and the Louisiana Territory.

Genêt believed Washington would have no choice but to sanction American participation in the French war with Britain and place his nation's military under the French flag—or step down in favor of Jefferson. Or perhaps Genêt himself

By then, Genêt's arrogance and ambitions knew no bounds, entwined as they were with restoration of French glory and encouraged by crowds of fanatic Francophiles.

"All the old spirit of 1776 is rekindling," Secretary of State Jefferson wrote with childish glee to his nephew as he continued equating Genêt's Jacobinism with liberty.

"A French frigate took a British prize off the capes of Delaware the other day and sent her up here," Jefferson exulted. "Upon her coming into sight, thousands and thousands of the yeomanry of the city crowded & covered the wharves. Never before was such a crowd seen here, and when the British colors were seen reversed & the French flag flying above, they burst into peals of joy."[63]

Anglophiles tried dismissing the impact of the incident and, indeed, of Genêt's presence in Philadelphia. "A crowd will always draw a crowd, whatever the purpose," scoffed Treasury Secretary Alexander Hamilton. Hamilton was openly contemptuous of Jefferson's embrace of French Jacobinism, calling any comparisons between the French and American revolutions "absurd," adding...

"Would to heaven we could discern in the mirror of French affairs the same humanity...the same order, the same dignity, the same solemnity which distinguished the American cause.... When I contemplate the horrid...massacres...when I perceive passion, tumult, and violence usurping reason and cool deliberation...I acknowledge that I am glad there is no resemblance between what was the cause of America and what is the case of France."[64]

Hamilton confronted Genêt, calling his actions offensive, only to hear Genêt fire back that Washington was guilty of misusing his executive powers by violating the terms of the Franco-American treaty and declaring the United States neutral.

When Jefferson finally escorted Genêt to President Washington's house for the long delayed formal presentation of his diplomatic credentials, the president reacted with unmistaken iciness.

13. French Minister Plenipotentiary Genêt resents his diplomatic credentials to President George Washington, as Secretary of State Thomas Jefferson looks on.

Although Genêt bowed obsequiously, he harbored nothing but scorn for the aging warrior, whom he described as having "an aristocratic or monarchical tendency."[65]

Genêt took advantage of what he perceived as a distinctly pro-French public bias by converting eight more American ships into French privateers. The promise of plunder from English and Spanish ships brought throngs of rowdy, beached seamen flocking to dockside to sail under the French flag.

After Britain threatened to declare war on the United States, Washington acted to end Genêt's activities with a set of "Rules Governing Belligerents," which prohibited foreign nations from arming privateers and recruiting American volunteers in United States territory. The president instructed Jefferson to notify Genêt that his grants of military commissions infringed on United States sovereignty and that he was to remove his ships from American waters.

By then, however, the secretary of state was so deeply involved with Genêt that he feared the Frenchman would reveal their connection. According to Genêt, Jefferson had already "initiated" him in "the foibles and secrets of your cabinet [and] political divisions of your country." According to Genêt, Jefferson had even told him he believed the president "was controlled by the English and the aristocrats" and that he, Jefferson, "was the only member of the Cabinet who still took an interest in France."[66]

Suddenly, Jefferson found himself in an untenable position exhibiting disloyalty to both the President and the nation and violating of his oath of office. Had he committed treason?

Chapter 9
'Washington Interferes with My Programs'

Without offering an explanation that went beyond an indiscretion of having befriended Genêt too warmly, Jefferson offered the President his resignation, but Washington insisted that he remain in the cabinet and, in effect, clean up the diplomatic mess he had created.

An embarrassed Jefferson went to Genêt with the presidential order to remove all French privateers from American waters and end sales of booty in American ports. Jefferson explained that Washington was exerting "the right of every nation to prohibit acts of sovereignty from being exercised by any other nation within its limits…[and] that the granting of military commissions within the United States by any other authority than their own is an infringement of their sovereignty."[67]

Genêt exploded with rage, charging President Washington with supporting "the king of England and other kings…to destroy the French republic and liberty….

"No one," he ranted, ""has the right to shackle our operations…. The French republicans, sir, know the duties which nations owe to one another. They know how to distinguish their enemies and their friends."[68]

Genêt's outburst stunned Jefferson. "He took up the subject in a very high tome and went into an immense field of declamation and complaint," the crestfallen Jefferson noted later. "I found it necessary to let him go on, and in fact could not do otherwise; for the few efforts which I made to take part in the conversation were quite ineffectual."[69]

Genêt went on to mock the president's order, proclaiming his [Genêt's] ships would continue to "seize every occasion" to attack British shipping.

By then, Genêt and his consuls in other major American cities had outfitted almost one hundred privateers, which, in the absence of an American navy, sailed in and out of American ports at will, in open violation of American law. They had captured more than eighty British merchant ships—many in American territorial waters. Almost every day saw riotous welcomes for every incoming privateer.

Unimpeded. French consuls sold captured ships and cargoes on the piers as American customs officials watched helplessly. In each port, Genêt ordered Jacobin clubs to offer free rum on the quays.

Washington countered Genêt's attempt to recruit Americans by ordering Attorney General Edmund Randolph to arrest any American seamen serving on French privateers when they stepped ashore. Sheriff's deputies did exactly that, arresting two American seamen when they disembarked in Philadelphia from the *Citizen Genêt* a privateer the French minister had modestly renamed for himself.

Genêt wrote an angry letter to Jefferson: "The crime of which they are accused, which my mind cannot conceive and my pen reluctantly records, is serving France, defending with her children the common and glorious cause of liberty."[70]

Charged with conspiring to attack the property and citizens of nations at peace with the United States, one of the men went to trial before the Federal Circuit Court of Philadelphia, with Genêt paying for his defense.

Although the judges (including two U.S. Supreme Court associate justices) ordered a jury verdict of guilty, Genêt bribed jurors to ensure the opposite.

Cheering members of Genêt's Jacobin Democratic Society led the sailor from the courthouse back to his ship to reenlist before attending a dinner that Genêt sponsored that evening to celebrate the young man's triumph over the federal government.

A second jury later found the second sailor innocent, with the defense attorney charging that the President's Neutrality Proclamation was unconstitutional and without the force of law. Instead of rallying Americans around their own flag, Washington's prosecution of two ordinary sailors further divided the nation and left him looking helpless to control the nation's course.

Ecstatic over his legal victories, Genêt exulted in a letter to his foreign minister in Paris:

"Washington," he wrote, "interferes with my programs in a thousand ways and obliges me to urge the convocation of Congress, the majority of which...will be decidedly in my favor."

In addition, Genêt added, "Jefferson...gave me useful notions of men in office and did not at all conceal from me that Senator [Robert] Morris and Secretary of the Treasury Hamilton influenced...the president's mind and that it was only with difficulty that he [Jefferson] counterbalanced their efforts. [71]

As a further insult to the president, Genêt ordered *The Little Sarah*, a British ship that his privateers had captured, refitted and armed under the President's nose in Philadelphia harbor.

Treasury Secretary Hamilton and Secretary of War Knox joined in expressing their outrage: "*The fitting out of privateers* in our ports by one of the belligerent powers...is an unequivocal breach of neutrality."[72]

Because the President in conformity with an unanimous opinion of the heads of departments and the attorney general...has caused his disapprobation of the practice to be signified to the ministers of both Great Britain and France...effectual measures would be taken to prevent a repetition of the practice.[73]

Hamilton and Knox went on to accuse Genêt with trying to implement "a plan to force the United States into the war" and "to endeavor to control the government itself by creating, if possible, a schism between it and the people and enlisting them on the side of France in opposition to their own constitutional authorities"

They called Genêt's recent note to Secretary of State Jefferson regarding the arrest of American sailors serving on French privateers "the most offensive paper, perhaps, that ever was offered by a foreign minister to a friendly power."[74]

Genêt answered in kind, angrily insisting in somewhat incomprehensible and often laughable "Franglish," that it was...

> *"...the incontestable right of the French Republic to fit out armed vessels in the ports of the United States, by virtue of the treaties of commerce and alliance subsisting between the two nations. It belongs to the French to determine whether to the sacrifices they have already made to your country, they ought to add that of renouncing a right, the exercise of which alarms the politics of your government and makes it apprehensive of being suspected of acting an underhand part in the war of Liberty."[75]*

Acting under the President's instructions, the governor of Pennsylvania ordered the ship detained.

Genêt sent an angry complaint to the French foreign minister in Paris saying that President Washington "interferes with my progress in a thousand ways and obliges me secretly to urge the convocation of Congress, the majority of which...will be in my favor."[76]

Genêt then told Pennsylvania's commonwealth secretary Alexander J. Dallas that he would appeal President Washington's decisions to "the real sovereigns of the United States—the people."[77]

Genêt thereupon resumed his insulting behavior by ordering *The Little Sarah* renamed *Petite Démocrate* and sent to sea to attack British ships. Although the governor considered firing on the vessel to prevent her leaving port, Jefferson intervened with a warning that it would be an act of war against France and that a powerful French fleet was approaching from Saint Domingue (the French portion of Santo Domingo, now Haiti). Jefferson explained his intervention by claiming that America could no more afford a war with France than it could with Britain.

But the *Petite Démocrate* nonetheless drew the United States closer to war with so many attacks on British ships that the British retaliated by seizing American cargo ships and impressing or imprisoning American seamen. Despite Washington's efforts to keep America neutral, war with Britain seemed inevitable unless he stopped Genêt.

After the *Petite Démocrate* had left, Genêt received a plea from George Rogers Clark for more French help attacking Spanish-held Louisiana.

Clark reported that widespread anger toward the Spanish among Kentucky frontiersmen had simplified the task of recruiting a western army. More than 2,000 had signed up after he had offered them 1,000-acre land grants in captured territory and 4,000 more had signed "intents."

Clark said his men would be ready to march once he received the appropriate commission for his officers, along with money for boats, guns, and ammunition.

After writing to France for further instructions, Genêt received this letter:

> *Kentuckians have long seethed with a legitimate desire to enjoy free navigation of the Mississippi—a natural right that you can help them acquire without compromising the Congress. The [French] executive council, therefore, authorizes Citizen Genêt*

> *to form and maintain a network of agents in Kentucky as well
> as Louisiana to execute the plans...to invade Spanish America
> and deliver our former brothers in Louisiana from the yoke of
> [Spanish] tyranny.*[78]

In accordance with his instructions, Genêt enlisted André Michaux, a renowned French botanist and fervent revolutionary to deliver funds for the George Rogers Clark expedition in Kentucky under the pretense of searching for new specimens.

Michaux had originally been appointed royal botanist by Louis XVI in 1785, and during the seven years that followed, he had sent 60,000 specimens of trees collected in Florida and the Bahamas back to France. He visited George Washington at Mount Vernon in 1786, then met with Jefferson and other members of the American Philosophical Society.

At Jefferson's request, the Society obtained a government *carte blanche* for Michaux "to explore the interior of North America from the Mississippi along the Missouri and westwardly to the Pacific ocean" on behalf of the Society.

In the spring of 1793, "Michaux had fallen under the spell of...Genêt, who convinced him to attempt to raise an American volunteer corps in Kentucky to aid in the liberation of Louisiana from Spanish rule."

Genêt gave Michaux instructions for Clark coordinating the Louisiana offensive with a French fleet that Genêt ordered to sail into the Gulf of Mexico to lay siege to New Orleans.

Although the French government had given Genêt only $60,000 to cover his own salary and expenses, it had assured him Jefferson would fund military expeditions by paying U.S. war debts to France in advance instead of annually.

Accordingly, Genêt laid out his plans for the Florida and Louisiana expeditions before the secretary of state, along with the formal requests for the American financial and military support he expected Jefferson to provide.

Genêt also asked Jefferson to waive Washington's neutrality proclamation and allow him to continue refitting captured ships as privateers, recruit seamen to man them, and sell the captured prizes in American ports.

"He called on me and read...an address to the inhab. of Louisiana & another to those of Canada," Jefferson reported in his notes on the meeting:

> *It appears that besides encouraging those inhabitants to insurrections, he speaks of two generals at Kentucky, who have proposed to him to go & take New Orleans if he will furnish the exp. About £3,000 sterl. He...proposes the officers shall be commissioned by himself in Kentucky & Louisiana, that they shall rendezvous out of the territories of the U.S. in Louisiana...and getting what Indians they could to undertake the expedition against New Orleans, and then Louisiana to be established as an independent state.*[79]

Jefferson now edged closer to treason by actively participating in the Genêt scheme and hiding it from the President. He wrote and gave the French botanist a warm letter of introduction to Kentucky Governor Isaac Shelby. Fully aware of the clandestine purpose of Michaux's mission, Jefferson used language that implied official U.S. government approval of the Clark expedition against the Spanish.

With Jefferson's diplomatic imprimatur in hand, Michaux left for Kentucky in mid-July. Jefferson then passed along Genêt's requests for arms, cannons, and money to the appropriate cabinet members.

Secretary of War Henry Knox, a fierce Washington loyalist, replied angrily that he would not lend Genêt so much as a pistol. Treasury

Secretary Hamilton reacted similarly, refusing to draw down a penny from Revolutionary War debts for the Genêt adventure.

Jefferson explained the refusals to Genêt in conciliatory tones, saying advance debt repayment would exhaust American government cash reserves and, in any event, was not required under terms of the original loans. He said the tiny American army could ill afford to spare a pistol, let alone the few cannons it owned.

He then lied to Genêt, saying that the government did not care what insurrections Genêt or his emissaries excited in Louisiana, but he warned that "enticing officers and soldiers from Kentucky to go against Spain was putting a halter about their necks, for they would assuredly be hung if they committed hostilities against a nation at peace with the United States."[80]

Jefferson's about-face infuriated Genêt, who charged the secretary of state with duplicity in having formerly espoused the French cause when he believed doing so would "win those tender objects of your desires...the great and lucrative posts of the Federal Government."[81]

Apparently abandoned by Jefferson, Genêt carried out his threat to appeal to the American people to rise against the Washington government. He expanded the number of "Democratic Clubs" to nearly forty and changed their stated mission from promoting Franco-American friendship to promising revolution, union with France, and war against Britain. He ordered them to infect the nation with pro-French war fever.

Like Jacobins in France, Genêt's agents infiltrated the American press and local political organizations, and, at a signal from Genêt, they filled streets with shrieking mobs and frightened newspaper readers with menacing headlines. The results terrified Washington supporters and proponents of neutrality.

"The freedom of this country," warned New York's *Columbian Gazeteer*, "is not secure until that of France is placed beyond the reach of accident."[82]

The *Baltimore Daily Repository* warned if European monarchs defeated France, "the craving appetite of despotism will be satisfied with nothing less than American vassalage in some form or another." Philadelphia's *General Advertiser* insisted that "the salvation of America depends on our alliance with France."[83]

Genêt waxed ecstatic as he wrote his report to the French foreign minister in Paris:

"Composed of the patriots of '76 [and] the most respectable citizens, the Democratic Societies have formed as if by magic from one end of the continent to the other, and set down as a foundation for their association these powerful words, *Liberté, Égalité, Fraternité*, Rights of Man, Country, France, Republic..... The [American] people voluntarily constituted themselves France's advocate."[84]

Genêt was ready to seize power.

Chapter 10
'The President
Was Much Inflamed.'

Genêt's ineluctable rise to power reached a peak on August 1. President Washington admitted as much, recognizing French warships in Philadelphia harbor for what they were: an occupying force.

Genêt all but confirmed Washington's assessment by blatantly skirting diplomatic protocol by treating directly with the President, without so much as a glance at Secretary of State Jefferson. It was an unheard of violation of diplomatic protocol by an ambassador to a head of state.

Dismissing Jefferson as a "limp puppet," Genêt sent Washington an ultimatum "in the name of France," demanding that the President call Congress into special session to choose between neutrality and war. Genêt seemed convinced that his command would ignite the street mobs and force the President to do his [Genêt's] bidding.

Genêt told the President that he believed "the sovereignty of the United States resides essentially in the people and its representatives in the Congress." He warned Washington if he refused to declare war on Britain, he—Genêt—would "appeal to the people...[the] decisions of the President."

He predicted that the "good, generous, grateful people [will] rally from all sides to support the envoy of the French people [and] demonstrate ...that the democrats of America realize perfectly that their fate is ultimately bound with ours."[85]

Genêt's ego seemed to know no bounds, and with his influence evolving into an ominously powerful movement, he sent the following note to Jefferson all-but-commanding the Secretary of State to commit treason. In a note unprecedented in American diplomatic history, Genêt ordered the following instructions from the French government "distributed among the members of Congress...

... and that you will request the President of the United States to lay them officially before both houses of that legislative body. This...will enable the representatives of the American people to determine whether my political conduct...has been conformable to... the interests of the United States."

Genêt then warned Jefferson and, indirectly, Washington, that if they failed to act on his demands, "nothing will remain for me but to prosecute in your courts of justice the authors and abettors of the odious and vile machinations that have been plotted against me...if not to break off entirely the alliance between two nations which every consideration calls upon to unite and rivet the bonds which tie them with each other."[86]

Washington reacted furiously, calling Genêt's political activities an "imminent danger to the Constitution." He accused Genêt's Democratic Societies and those still calling themselves Jefferson clubs of planning "the subversion of the government of these states, even at the expense of plunging the country into the horrors of a disastrous war."[87]

As Genêt's mobs held Philadelphia in thrall, the Frenchman crossed a line of rational, not to mention diplomatic, behavior by barging into a presidential reception and demanding an immediate interview with the President.

To avoid a public confrontation and scandal, the President led the intruder into a private study, where Genêt urged Washington "to put yourself in my place and consider by your proclamation of neutrality...you have annulled the most sacred treaties, taken from the French people at a time when it had the greatest need of it in order to defend its colonies, an alliance which it looked upon as a possession dearly bought; you would agree that unless I were a traitor, I could not act otherwise."[88]

Genêt's interview with the President went so far beyond the bounds of diplomatic protocol that Washington took no formal notes. Genêt alone commented that "the President listened to everything and said to me simply that it was of very slight importance to him whether his administration was talked about. We went out; he accompanied me as far as the stairs, took my hand and shook it."[89]

The next day, Genêt approached his puppet Jefferson and "used every method to find out if the President has spoken to you of my efforts, but you were impenetrable."

Knowing he faced accusations of disloyalty and even charges of treason, Jefferson berated Genêt for having dared approach the President directly.

Then, suddenly, Washington flung open the door and marched into the Secretary of State's office. Genêt stood and "looked from one to the other to see if I might read in your eyes an invitation to remain...but a very imperative sign from you forced me to retire."[90]

The President told Jefferson of having read accusations in the Hamiltonian press that he—Jefferson—was in the pay of the French government and, in effect, committing treason.

Jefferson again offered his resignation. This time, the President accepted, but insisted that Jefferson remain until the end of the year to make the departure seem less the result of treasonous activities related to Genêt. Washington made it clear he was about to clean his administrative house.

"It is my desire," the President later wrote in a noticeably hostile note to Jefferson, "that all communications to and from that minister [Genêt] be laid before me.... I therefore desire you will bring with you all his letters, your answers, and such other papers as are connected with the subject."[91]

With that, Jefferson's influence in the cabinet ended, and he began focusing on efforts to disassociate himself from Genêt and avoid charges of complicity in the attempted overthrow of the U.S. government.

"I am doing everything in my power," he wrote to his acolyte James Monroe, "to moderate his impetuosity...and to destroy the dangerous opinion...that the people of the United States will disavow the acts of their government, and that he has an appeal from the Executive to the Congress and from both to the people."[92]

With Jefferson's resignation in view, the President himself assumed control of foreign affairs. At a cabinet meeting the next day, Washington announced his intention to demand that the French government recall Genêt, saying that "the best that can be said of this agent [Genêt] is that he is entirely unfit for the mission on which he is employed [and]...contrary to the express & unequivocal declaration of his country...."[93]

President Washington then asked for cabinet member opinions on whether Democratic Societies presented enough of a menace to warrant a ban on their activities.

Hamilton spoke first, calling them Jacobins paid by Genêt and the French government to undermine the American government. Secretary of War Henry Knox concurred and read an article from a pamphlet attacking Washington's "aristocratic or monarchical tendencies"—words Jefferson recognized as Genêt's. Jefferson took notes:

> *The Presdt. was much inflamed, got into one of those passions when he cannot command himself, ran on much on the personal abuse which had been bestowed on him, defied any man on earth to produce a single act of his since he had been*

in government which has not been done on the purest motives...that by God he had rather be in his grave than in his present situation; that he had rather be on his farm than to be made emperor of the world; and yet they were charging him with wanting to be a king...that he could see in this nothing but an impudent design to insult him. He ended in this high tone.[94]

As Washington sat by himself in the presidential mansion later, he ruminated over his infuriating lack of power to respond to Genêt's provocations. Genêt's fleet of privateers had captured more than 80 British merchant vessels—many inside American territorial waters—and sailed them into American ports to be sold by French consuls.

Genêt ordered Jacobin clubs in each port to offer free rum on the quays to ensure riotous welcomes for every privateer and to menace any American officials who even breathed a word of protest.

To the cheers of thousands, one French privateer sailed into Boston harbor with a banner flying from its mast listing eleven prominent Bostonians as "aristocrats" and "enemies of France."

Genêt made a show of personal defiance of Washington's Neutrality Proclamation when his own flagship, *l'Embuscade,* captured a British vessel in Delaware Bay—well within American territorial waters—and sailed up to Philadelphia with the British boat in tow, its flag flying upside down to humiliate the British and Americans. Not only was Washington's presidency collapsing, so was the American union.

Chapter 11
'The Freedom of This Country Is Not Secure'

Genêt took full advantage of the turmoil he had generated in Philadelphia by converting eight more American ships into French privateers in local dockyards. The alterations put hundreds of grateful ship fitters to work, while the promise of plunder from English and Spanish ships lured throngs of rowdy American seamen and would-be seamen to dockside to enlist in Genêt's service.

After Britain threatened to declare war on the United States for the French attacks, Washington issued a set of "Rules Governing Belligerents," which prohibited Genêt and other foreigners from recruiting Americans for foreign wars and outfitting privateers on American territory.

The President then instructed Jefferson to notify Genêt that his grants of military commissions infringed on United States sovereignty and that he was to remove his ships from American waters.

By then, however, Jefferson had expressed such open support for Genêt that he was caught in a political vice. Declaring Genêt a friend of the United States, Jefferson dismissed the dangers of pro-French riots on the waterfront as nothing more than "the old spirit of 1776 rekindling."[95] But Washington recognized Genêt's ships for what they were—an occupying force that Genêt was using to try to dictate American policy.

He called an emergency session of the cabinet and exploded with anger. Was Genêt "to set the acts of this government at defiance with impunity?" he thundered. "What must the world think of such conduct, and of the government...submitting to it? We are an independent nation. We will not be dictated to by the politics of any nation under heaven."[96]

Washington accused Jefferson and his Democratic Clubs of planning "nothing short of the subversion of the government of these states, even at the expense of plunging this country in the horrors of a disastrous war."[97]

Washington now expressed open opposition to the French Revolution. All his closest French friends from America's Revolutionary War, including Lafayette, were aristocrats. Indeed, almost all the heroic French officers of the American Revolution were aristocrats, and the members of America's own officer corps, including Washington, were largely the equivalent of an American landed aristocracy. He had no difficulty imagining a blood bath in America if Jefferson's Francophilic street mobs gained control of political power.

Although American mobs had been ruthless in their use of tar and feathers during tax protests, they had stopped short of outright butchery. French mobs routinely disemboweled their victims alive or hacked off their heads and other body parts to plant on pikes for display in street parades.

Jefferson made a serious *faux pas* bringing a pro-French newspaper to a cabinet meeting. Its headline accused Washington of "monarchical ambitions" and illustrated the article that followed with a cartoon showing Washington's head on the pavement after being severed by a guillotine blade.

Considering it a silent warning by his Secretary of State, Washington snapped—-erupting with an angry outburst that few had ever witnessed

Jefferson said the President shouted that if anyone tried to introduce monarchy in America, "no man would set his face against it more...that there was more danger of anarchy being introduced...the president was evidently sore and warm."[98]

In fact, the President was more than "sore and warm." He was irate and all but irrational in his fury. Beset by personal problems, he had reached the end of his patience and ability to deal objectively with the overwhelming number of public and private crises he now faced. Instead of helping ease the Presidential burden as Hamilton did, Jefferson seemed ready to do nothing but add to those burdens. In truth, Jefferson all but loathed the President, saying Washington "could not brook contradiction."

"I have long thought it was best," Jefferson told an acquaintance, "to soothe him [Washington] by flattery."[99]

Earlier in the year, the French Revolutionary Government had declared Lafayette an enemy of the French Revolution. Washington was stunned. When Lafayette was but 19, his heroics in America's Revolutionary War won the admiration and heart of Washington, who all but adopted the French boy as his own.

Now forced to flee revolutionaries in his native France, Lafayette had only just crossed the French border when Austrian troops seized him and threw him into prison for complicity in having started the French Revolution and set loose French mobs streaming across French borders to loot and pillage neighboring lands and overthrow ruling monarchs.

To add to Washington's woes, his favorite nephew George Augustine Washington had died of tuberculosis. The young man had fought gallantly in the Revolution before marrying Martha Washington's niece Fanny. He left her widowed, still-young, with three infant children.

Fanny's mother had died when Fanny was 12, and he and Martha had raised Fanny as their own. They had been thrilled when she married Washington's favorite nephew.

"My dear Fanny," the grieving President now wrote. "It is unnecessary to describe the sorrow with which I was afflicted at the news of his death.... To express sorrow with the force I feel it would answer no purpose ....The object of this present letter is to convey to your mind the warmest assurances of my love, friendship, and disposition to serve you. These also I profess to have...for your children. I know not what plans you have contemplated...the one that strikes me most favorably...is to return to Mount Vernon. You can go to no place where you will be more welcome...." And he signed it with "love to the children–and with affectionate sentiments" to her.[100]

Shortly thereafter, Fanny and her three children moved into the mansion at Mount Vernon, adding three more children to the five orphaned children the Washingtons were already raising at the plantation—at the age of 61.

It was little wonder that Washington snapped when Jefferson showed him a cartoon disparaging the President and showing him on the guillotine about to lose his head.

Accused of disloyalty and humiliated at the cabinet meeting, Jefferson again offered the President his resignation, but the President raged at his secretary of state, demanding that he remain in office until the end of the year and fulfil his oath of office by transmitting the presidential order for Genêt to remove his warships.

Although Genêt was furious at Washington's order, he was, for the first time in America, helpless to respond. He had arrived with only 60,000 livres, or slightly more than $10,000–far from enough to raise an army.

The French foreign ministry had assured him that Jefferson would fund his expeditions with American government arms, ammunition, and cash. But with no funds, arms, or ammunition at his disposal, Jefferson, adroitly side-stepped his entanglement by passing along the Frenchman's requests for funds to Secretary of War Henry Knox and, of all people, to Treasury Secretary Hamilton.

Knox replied angrily that he would not lend Genêt so much as a pistol, while Hamilton reacted with equal furor by refusing Genêt even a penny of American money.

When Jefferson refused to intercede, Genêt charged the Secretary of State with duplicity and expanded his direct appeals to the American people.

Accordingly, Genêt ordered leaders of his Democratic Societies to change their mission from promoting Franco-American friendship to promoting revolution in America and ultimate union with France. Like Jacobins in France, they had already infiltrated the press and local political establishments. At a signal from Genêt, they could fill the streets with shrieking mobs and provoke frightening newspaper headlines.

"The freedom of this country," claimed New York's *Columbian Gazeteer*, "is not secure until that of France is placed beyond the reach of accident."[101]

The *Baltimore Daily Repository* warned that if Europe's monarchs defeated France, "the craving appetite of despotism will be satisfied with nothing less than American vassalage in some form or another."

Philadelphia's *General Advertiser* insisted that "the salvation of America depends on our alliance with France."[102]

Genêt waxed ecstatic in his report to the Foreign Ministry in Paris:

"Composed of the patriots of '76 and the most respectable citizens," he wrote, "the Democratic Societies have formed as if by magic from one end of the continent to the other, and set down as a foundation for their association these powerful words: Liberty, Equality, Rights of Man, Country, France, Republic…. The American people voluntarily constitute themselves France's advocate."[103]

Reports in the Hamiltonian press that Jefferson was in the pay of the French government convinced Washington that Jefferson was too torn between his allegiance to the French Revolution and his obligations to serve the United States.

It was not the first time Jefferson had deceived Washington. In helping write the Declaration of Independence, Jefferson had ended that document with a pledge to sacrifice "our Lives, our Fortunes, and our sacred Honor" in the fight for independence. But after signing it, he had galloped off to the safety of his 5,000-acre mountain aerie in the woods of far-off Charlottesville, Virginia—far from the battlegrounds where Washington risked his life with those of his men.. Though governor of his state and a colonel in the Virginia militia, Jefferson failed to fire a single shot during the eight-year revolution that he helped incite.

Even some of his closest colleagues in the state assembly mocked him and began impeachment proceedings against him until news of Washington's Yorktown victory interrupted proceedings and sent delegates into raptures of joy and celebratory reels along the aisles. By the time they stopped, Jefferson had resigned the governorship and galloped home to his mountain-top retreat.

Now, without warning Jefferson, Washington told his cabinet that he had acted independently of the Secretary of State and demanded Genêt's recall by the French government.

He then asked for opinions on whether to ban Democratic Societies, whose numbers by then had grown to well over 40.

Hamilton charged that their members were paid by Genêt and the French Government to provoke anti-government sentiment. Knox agreed, but Washington argued that outlawing the societies would only incite defenders of the Bill of Rights.

He decided, instead, to rely on the imminent recall of Genêt and Jefferson's departure from government to quiet the Democratic Societies as well. In the meantime, Washington demanded that Jefferson reveal all his notes. Now it was Jefferson's turn to feign anger, saying he refused to open his private notes to public display, but backed down when Washington agreed to keep the notes confidential.

Meanwhile, Genêt had abandoned hope for cooperation from the American government. He ordered the French fleet to sail to New

York for repairs and resupply before dividing into three squadrons for assaults on Canada, Florida, and Louisiana.

L'Embuscade led the triumphant French fleet into New York harbor, huge banners streaming from her masts: "Enemies of equality: Reform or tremble!" read the banner on the foremast. "Freemen, Behold! We are your friends and brothers!" flew from the mainmast. "We are armed for the defense of the Rights of Man!" waved from the mizzen.

After the ships had put into port, more than 5,000 French sailors and marines spilled over the rails of the French fleet and joined the city's Jacobins and Francophiles in an endless orgy of drunkenness and violence that all but leveled the waterfront's tumbledown warehouses.

Meanwhile, Tories and their families joined a long train of carriages fleeing the city tumult and the constant, unnerving, monotonous French revolutionary chant,

> *Ah, ça ira, ça ira, ça ira;*
> *Les aristocrats à la lantern;*
> *Ah, ça ira, ça ira, ça ira;*
> *Les aristocrats, on les pendra.*[S]

A week later–on August 7—Genêt himself arrived dressed in his adjutant general's uniform, ready to mobilize cheering Americans to unseat the President. The hysterical mobs did nothing to dissuade him. Indeed, they serenaded him with revolutionary airs and chanted, "Genêt to power!" "Down with Washington!"

Cannon fire and church bells added resonance to their welcome.

Then the crowd swept him away on an endless series of unruly parades through Manhattan's narrow streets, barking their frenzied calls for revolution in counterpoint to the incessant thunder claps of church bells. Adoring women leaned from windows, cheering his every step, pledging to follow the handsome young Frenchman into battle—into hell if necessary.

Pro-French editors welcomed Genêt with front-page headlines. "Americans are ready to mingle their most precious blood with yours," began one front-page article.

Newspaper cartoonists portrayed the heads of American political leaders dropping from guillotine scaffolds.

One cartoonist showed Vice President Adams embracing "a stinking prostitute" with the face of Washington. Another showed Chief Justice John Jay leading royalist plotters in seating "King Washington" on the American throne.

Another showed Genêt tearing a crown off the President's head.[104]

Washington fumed that he needed a permanent law enforcement arm if he was to maintain order, but the Constitution, in assigning him to execute the laws–"faithfully"—gave him no mechanism for doing so. For the moment he was helpless to prevent Genêt from staging a *coup d'état.*

"The whole of America has risen to acknowledge me," Genêt exulted. At thirty years of age, he was ready to raise the French flag over New York, reclaim New France, and restore his nation's glory in the Americas.

At a dinner hosted by New York's ardent Antifederalist governor George Clinton, Genêt declared that "the cause of France is the cause of mankind." All but swooning at his words was the governor's daughter Cornelia, who had canonized the butchers of the French Revolution and fell instantly in love with Genêt.

The next morning, August 15, Genêt issued what he knew were worthless drafts totaling $100,000 to local shipbuilders to repair and refit the fleet. As church bells pealed, he climbed aboard his flagship dressed in full military regalia to issue orders for the assaults on

Halifax, St. Augustine, and New Orleans once the repairs were complete. On the quays below, a crowd formed to serenade him:

Liberty! Liberty! Be thy name adored forever;
Tyrants beware! Your tott'ring thrones must fall;

Our int'rest links the free together,

And Freedom's sons are Frenchmen all.[105]

By midday, however, the volume of the chant had diminished; one by one, members of the crowd had darted off the pier, and one by one, the church bells had ceased their incessant ringing. By 1:00 in the afternoon, an eerie calm had settled over the waterfront.

As the atmosphere about the ship waxed silent, Genêt came topside and looked over the rail. The waterfront was deserted; the air still and silent.

He disembarked and walked toward the inn where he had dined several times. A servant stood at the door, his bag packed to leave. Genêt demanded an explanation. The answer struck like a dagger:

"Yellow fever, Monsieur."

"The coolest and the firmest minds," John Adams recalled later, "have given their opinions that nothing but the yellow fever...could have saved the United States from a fatal revolution of government."[106]

Had the epidemic arrived a month later, Genêt's armies would have invaded Florida, Canada, and Louisiana; he himself would have roused his Jacobin legions in New York, Boston, and Philadelphia and marched into the capital to unseat, perhaps execute, President Washington and raise Jefferson to a seat of absolute power in the United States.

On August 15, however, the terrible, swift Yellow Fever infection sent New Yorkers and Philadelphians—Jacobins and non-Jacobins alike–fleeing by the thousands to the perceived safety of the countryside. Life came to a standstill in major cities. The entire government shut down in Philadelphia, with the Washingtons and their herd of children going home to their isolated country seat at Mount Vernon.

Before the first autumn frosts arrived to kill the offending mosquitoes that carried the disease, the French sailors mutinied after learning that Genêt planned sending them to war and had no funds to pay them.

As they seized control of each of Genêt's ships, Genêt pleaded with them, shouted patriotic slogans, spoke of loyalty to the nation, to the Revolution, to the Republic—all for naught.

The mutineers were resolute. When he ordered officers to disarm the mutineers, they turned their backs on him and ordered their crews to cast off and sail home to France.

To add to his indignities, Genêt ran out of funds to pay for his own keep and, having failed to obtain the advance repayments of U.S. wartime debts to France from Hamilton, he was unable to pay his personal debts to merchants in Boston, New York, Philadelphia, Charleston, and elsewhere.

As newspapers reported Genêt's insolvency, Hamilton wrote a newspaper article exposing Genêt's threat to appeal the President's decisions to the people.

Using the pen name, "No Jacobin," Hamilton bitterly attacked Genêt, decrying "the very disrespectful treatment we have experienced from the agents of France, who have acted towards us from the beginning more like a dependent colony than an independent nation."[107]

Even staunch Francophiles now turned on Genêt for plotting "to bring down the federal government...and incite insurrection, riot, and treason."[108]

Stunned by attacks in newspapers that had once heralded his virtues, Genêt wrote an angry letter to the President demanding that he disparage the "dark calumnies" and issue "an explicit declaration that I have never intimated to you an intention of appealing to the people."[109]

Under orders from Washington, Secretary of State Jefferson, now thoroughly cowed by the President, answered Genêt's letter, writing,

> "I am desired to observe to you that it is not the established course for the diplomatic characters residing here to have any direct correspondence with him [the President]. The Secretary of State is the organ through which their communications should pass."[110]

By then, President Washington's patience with Genêt had ended, and he sent another formal demand to the French government for Genêt's recall. To avoid conflict with France, he ordered Jefferson to draw "a clear line between him [Genêt] and his nation, expressing our friendship to the latter, but insisting on the recall." Jefferson's letter explained the President's position in blunt terms:

> "When the [U.S.] government forbids their citizens to arm and engage in war, he [Genêt] undertakes to arm and engage them. When they forbid vessels to be fitted in ports...he commissions them to fight and cruise. When they forbid an unceded jurisdiction to be exercised within their territory, he undertakes to uphold that exercise and to avow it openly."[111]

Fearful that Genêt might retaliate by inciting a Jacobin rebellion, the cabinet postponed notifying him of the recall for a month after they had sent it to France—too late for him to commandeer a ship to intercept it. Jefferson did not give Genêt a copy until mid-September.

Clearly taken aback but not humbled—never humbled!—Genêt nonetheless realized that the departure of the fleet and dispersal of Jacobin mobs had left him powerless to respond with arms. He therefore sent Jefferson an audacious letter renewing his threat to appeal to the American people.

Fearfully embarrassed, with his political career evidently at an end because of his ties to the Frenchman, Jefferson tried distancing himself by accusing Genêt of having conducted himself as if he were "a co-sovereign."

In a disingenuous letter to James Madison, by then the Republican leader in Congress, Jefferson denounced Genêt for having "thrown down the gauntlet to the President....

> *"I believe it will be true wisdom in the Republican party...to abandon Genêt entirely, [but] with expressions of strong friendship and adherence to his nation.... In this way we shall keep the people on our side.... I have been myself under a cruel dilemma with him. I adhered to him as long as I could...[but] finding at length that the man was absolutely incorrigible...I saw the necessity of quitting a wreck which would but sink all who should cling to it."[112]*

At Madison's suggestion, Jefferson tried salvaging his own reputation with a curt reply to Genêt that the Republicans in Congress would not consider his appeal.

As fearful as Jefferson was of being charged with treason, South Carolina Governor Moultrie, Genêt's earliest American champion, also tried cutting ties to the Frenchman to avoid charges of treason. Indeed, Moultrie now contended that Genêt's insults to the President had offended and alienated all the friends that France had once claimed in America.

Unfortunately, Genêt believed that his conduct had simply reflected the views of the bloodthirsty Jacobins in France and their venomous leader, the lawyer Maximilien Robespierre.

Although Robespierre's followers lusted for foreign conquest even more than their predecessors, they also faced the immediate task of feeding their nation after a devastating, long-lasting drought had left the nation's farms all but barren and the nation's people facing starvation.

The United States remained France's lone ally and only major source of imported foodstuffs. Recognizing his nation's need for American help, Robespierre grew incensed when he learned of Genêt's conduct and ordered his immediate recall.

No longer intimidated by Genêt's co-conspirators, Washington revoked the accreditation of the French vice-consul in Boston for ordering an armed patrol to free a French privateer from American custody.

On Washington's orders, Jefferson sent a letter to all other French consuls threatening the same fate if they failed to comply with American laws. Every French official feared such a fate and the head-wrenching consequences they would face if sent home to France.

Genêt continued peppering Congress with letters questioning presidential authority, but when Congress reconvened in December, it referred all his documents to Jefferson without a reading. Jefferson, in turn, returned the correspondence to Genêt with a curt warning to stop meddling in American government affairs. Henceforth, he added, the American government would await his replacement for any further diplomatic intercourse.

Anxious to bury any evidence of what may have been painted as treasonous complicity with Genêt, Jefferson rained letters on the press and his political allies, calling Genêt "hot headed" and pretending never to have embraced the Frenchman or his ideas.

He wrote to Madison, calling Genêt "all imagination, no judgment; passionate, disrespectful & even indecent towards the P[resident] in his written as well as verbal communications talking of appeals to Congress, from them to the people, urging the most unreasonable & groundless propositions & in the most dictatorial style, & c, & c, & c."[113]

In contrast, documents in the Archives of the French Ministry of Foreign Affairs in Paris show Genêt to have been both rational and exceptionally knowledgeable about the American political system. Indeed, he appears to have had no less an understanding of American government than Jefferson.

In fact, Genêt had studied the workings of the American and many other political systems for more than fifteen years under the tutelage of the most experienced diplomats in the western world—his father, the French master spy. He had, therefore, no illusions about America's system of government before the American Revolution, during the Confederation, and after enactment of the Constitution.

Far from irrational or ignorant about American politics, Genêt was a cold, calculating, and experienced agent of the sophisticated French secret service, with superior training for more than a decade in diplomacy, espionage, and crowd management—and fanatically dedicated to implementing his nation's policy of territorial conquest and world domination.

In the end, Genêt followed his government's instructions to the letter, using feigned mercurial behavior as a calculated tool to terrorize timid American officials to do his bidding.

Even the British ambassador at the time, George Hammond, agreed that "however intemperate, reprehensible, and unwarrantable his conduct may have been, he has not essentially exceeded the spirit of his instructions."[114]

On December 31, 1793, Jefferson resigned from office and retired to his isolated hilltop plantation in Charlottesville, Virginia. His withdrawal ended the deepest division that had ever developed in Washington's cabinet, but left the President in firm control of administration policies.

To Washington's relief, a new French ambassador, Jean-Antoine-Joseph Fauchet, arrived in Philadelphia a month later.

After conforming to strict diplomatic protocol by immediately presenting his credentials to the President, he gave Washington's secretary of state-designate, Attorney General Edmund Randolph, a French-government warrant for the arrest of Citizen Edmond Charles Genêt "to bring him back to France aboard one of the French ships in port and force him to account for his conduct towards an ally whose friendship and esteem are so dear to the French government."[115]

Although Vice-President Adams despised Genêt, he recoiled at the fate awaiting the Frenchman. "Poor Genêt, I fear, is undone, he wrote to his wife Abigail. "Bad as his conduct has been, I cannot but pity him. What will become of him, I know not."[116]

Chapter 12

'The Insidious Wiles of Foreign Influence'

In one of his first acts, the new French ambassador to the United States, revoked the French military commissions Genêt had issued. He then warned all French citizens against acting in any way to violate American neutrality.

Although the revocation ended one crisis, it was almost as embarrassing to the President as Genêt's original issuance of commissions. In one stroke of his pen, a French foreign envoy had done in a few minutes what the President's threats and decrees had failed to do in a year. In effect, Fauchet had exposed to the world America's presidential impotence and subservience to a foreign power.

In the weeks that followed, Genêt's military squads gradually disbanded, and Ambassador Fauchet tried without success to implement his warrant for Citizen Genêt's arrest. Genêt pleaded with the new Secretary of State Edmund Randolph not to enforce the warrant.

All but sobbing, the once defiant Genêt told Randolph that a former Paris police chief was waiting below deck on Fauchet's ship, sharpening the blade on a small, on-board guillotine to sever Genêt's neck before the ship even sailed.

A former Virginia governor and close friend of Washington, Randolph turned to the President for guidance. Even Hamilton now relented, saying Washington should not risk his own reputation as a great humanitarian by sending Genêt to his death.

"We ought not to wish his punishment," Washington decided, and granted the Frenchman political asylum and the protection of the government he had reviled and tried to overthrow.[117]

Fearing correctly that Fauchet's agents would try to kidnap him, Genêt sneaked out of Philadelphia during the night, unnoticed by the very Jacobin agents he had recruited to spread turmoil in the American capital.

He found his way to a secluded hideaway on a friend's farm in Bristol, Connecticut, where he temporarily disappeared from public view—with good reason. The Robespierre regime in France had by then sent an estimated 40,000 dissidents to the guillotine without trial; Genêt knew what his fate would be if he tried to return to his homeland. Although his name continued appearing in the press from time to time—usually reviled for his seditious activities—he remained out of sight until July 4, 1794.

To the astonishment of New York celebrants, the arrogant chameleonic Frenchman who tried to overturn the American government reappeared in New York's Independence Day parade marching arm-in-arm with Republican governor George Clinton and the governor's daughter Cornelia, a rabid republican who shared Genêt's revolutionary fantasies.

Along the parade route, members of New York's Democratic Societies cheered his unexpected reappearance. Whether it was while they marched together or shortly thereafter, Genêt asked for and won Cornelia's hand.

A handsome dowry from her father allowed him to buy a 325-acre farm near Jamaica, Mew York. Under the governor's protection, Genêt became an American citizen and settled into the life of an American gentleman farmer—a *cultivateur américain,* as he put it in his letters to his sisters in France. He nonetheless resumed writing insanely angry, albeit anonymous, newspaper articles denouncing the American government.

14. Cornelia Clinton Genêt.

By then, news of indiscriminate mass executions on French guillotines by Robespierre's Jacobin government had reached the American public, and even the most fervent American Francophiles turned against America's homemade Jacobin clubs.

Washington denounced them for sowing "the seeds of the people's jealousy and distrust of the government." He called the Jacobin clubs in the U.S. "the most diabolical attempt to destroy the best fabric of human government and happiness that has ever been presented for the acceptance of mankind." He blamed Genêt for having "brought the eggs of these venomous reptiles to our shores."[118]

15. Even as a retired gentleman farmer, Edmond Genêt did not cease issuing anti-government diatribes to the press.

The President's attack had its desired effect; the Democratic Societies and Jacobin Clubs stopped publishing Genêt's diatribes.

Although Jefferson had also slipped away into temporary political obscurity, he, unlike Genêt, had not abandoned his political ambitions or his flirtation with treason.

In an all-but-treasonous letter he sent to his friend, Virginia wine producer Filippo Mazzei, he vilified Washington and Hamilton as "apostates who have gone over to heresies, men who were Samsons in the field and Solomons in the councils, but who have had their heads shorn by the harlot England.

In place of that noble love of liberty & republican government which carried us triumphantly thro' the war, an Anglican, monarchical & aristocratical party has sprung up, whose avowed object is to draw over us...the forms of the British government…. Against us are the Executive, the Judiciary…all the officers of the government, all who want to be officers, all timid men who prefer calm despotism to the boisterous sea of liberty, British merchants & Americans trading on British capital, speculators & holders in the banks & public funds, a contrivance for the purposes of corruption & and for assimilating us in all things, to the rotten as well as the sound parts of the British model."[119]

—-

Although the Genêt affair had shaken the presidential structure, the Frenchman's retreat to Long Island and Jefferson's resignation and retreat to Charlottesville, Virginia, left Washington's presidency intact for the moment.

Washington acted immediately to tighten structural supports, but suffered still another political—and personal—blow after a British frigate captured a sloop carrying the papers of Jean Antoine Fauchet. The French ambassador who had succeeded Genêt had been returning to France after completing his American assignment when the British intercepted him.

Among the captured Fauchet papers was a copy of a Fauchet letter to the French foreign minister reporting that Secretary of State Randolph had solicited bribes from the French ambassador to disclose terms of a new treaty of commerce between the United States and Great Britain, which had been before the U.S. Senate for consideration.

"Mr. Randolph came to see me with a countenance of much anxiety and made me the overtures of which I have given you an account," Fauchet wrote in the letter, which newspapers across Britain and America republished in bold letters on their front pages.

The letter staggered Washington, who had known and trusted his fellow Virginian for years and considered him a close personal friend. A wealthy plantation owner like Washington, he had been Washington's aide-de-camp in Boston in 1775 before becoming Virginia governor.

The President all but broke down in tears. First Jefferson; now Randolph...it was all too much.

Concluding that Randolph had pocketed thousands of dollars, Washington showed the letter to Randolph and although Randolph denied accepting money from Fauchet, he resigned. Newspapers called the letter final proof of treachery by the French government, the Democratic Societies, and American Francophiles—all of it initiated by Genêt.

On September 19, 1796, Washington announced he would retire at the end of his second term instead of seeking re-election. The turmoil surrounding the Genêt affair and its aftermath had exhausted him, and the barrage of personal attacks had wounded him deeply.

In his "Farewell Address," to the American people, the President prayed "that your Union and brotherly affection may be perpetual; that your Constitution, which is the work of your hands, may be sacredly maintained." He warned against "the insidious wiles of foreign influence."[120]

George Washington's retirement from public office fired Thomas Jefferson's political ambitions. Although he finished second to John Adams in the 1796 presidential elections, second place—at that time—entitled him to seize the vice-presidency—a seat he used to try to undermine the federal government.

In an anonymous proposal to the Kentucky legislature, he obtained passage of a state resolution that individual states had the right and power to reject as "null and void" any federal legislation they deemed an exercise of undelegated constitutional authority.

"My idea," Jefferson contended, "is that we should be made one nation in...foreign affairs & separate ones in whatever is merely domestic."[121]

By then, Jefferson had seduced his protégé James Madison to force a similar resolution through the Virginia legislature. But when, in 1800, Jefferson won election to the presidency and appointed Madison his secretary of state, the two did an about-face, taking a tight hold of the reins of power and imposing so strict a federalist regime that they plunged the United States into a second—and totally unnecessary—war with Britain in 1812.

Edmond Charles Genêt, meanwhile, led the rest of his life far from the political mainstream on his farm, where he died and was buried unceremoniously at the age of 71—on Bastille Day, July 14, 1834.

Genêt fathered six children by Cornelia Clinton. One great-great grandson, Edmund Charles Clinton Genêt, became a heroic American pilot with the Lafayette Escadrille, a group of American fliers who volunteered to fight with the allies in World War I before the United States entered the war. He was the first American aviator killed in that war–shot down in the skies over his great-great grandfather's native France.

1. Edmond-Charles Genêt's great-great grandson,

was a heroic pilot in World War I—the first
American aviator to die in that conflict.

Appendix

Washington's Neutrality Proclamation

[Note: There are two types of presidential proclamations: "ceremonial" and "substantive." The first, *without* the force of law, often designates a national holiday; the second, *with* the force of law, usually relates to international trade or the use of federal lands. Although President Washington had issued several ceremonial proclamations—he declared Thanksgiving Day a national holiday, for example—the Neutrality Proclamation of April 22, 1793 cited below was the first "substantive" proclamation in American history.]

WHEREAS it appears that a state of war exists between Austria, Prussia, Sardinia, Great Britain, and the United Netherlands on the one part, and France on the other, and the duty and interest of the United States require, that they should with sincerity and good faith adopt and pursue a conduct friendly and impartial toward the belligerent powers:

I have therefore thought fit by these presents to declare the disposition of the United States to observe the conduct aforesaid towards those powers respectively; and to exhort and warn the citizens of the United States carefully to avoid all acts and proceedings whatsoever, which may in any manner tend to contravene such disposition.

And I do hereby make known that whosoever of the citizens of the United States shall render himself liable to punishment or forfeiture under the law of nations, by committing, aiding or abetting hostilities against any of the said powers, or by carrying to any of them those articles, which are deemed contraband in the *modern* usage of nations, will not receive the protection of the United States, against such punishment or forfeiture; and further, that I have given instructions to those officers, to whom it belongs, to cause prosecutions to be instituted against all persons who shall, with the cognizance of the courts of the United States, violate the Law of Nations, with respect to the powers at war, or any of them.

IN TESTIMONY WHEREOF I have caused the Seal of the United States of America to be affixed to these presents, and signed the same with my hand.

Done at the city of Philadelphia, the twenty-second day of April, one thousand seven hundred and ninety-three, and the Independence of the United States of America the seventeenth.

Go. WASHINGTON.

By the President.

Th: Jefferson.

Bibliography

Henry Ammon, *The Genêt Mission* (New York: Norton & Co., 1973).

Henry Budd, *Citizen Genêt's Visit to Philadelphia* (Philadelphia: City History Society of Philadelphia, 1918.)

Ron Chernow, *Alexander Hamilton* (New York: The Penguin Press, 2004).

Edward S. Corwin, *French Policy and the American Alliance* (Gloucester, MA: Peter Smith, 1969).

Alexander DeConde, *Entangling Alliance* (Durham, NC: Duke University Press, 1958).

Henri Doniol, *Histoire de la Participation de la France à l'Établissement des États-Unis d'Amérique* (Paris: Imprimerie Nationale, 1886, 5 vols., quarto)

[Edmond Charles Genêt,] *The Correspondence between Citizen Genêt...and the Officers of the Federal Government...Instructions from the Constituted Authorities of France* (Philadelphia: Benjamin Franklin Bache, 1793).

George Clinton Genêt, *Washington, Jefferson and "Citizen" Genêt, 1793* (New York: privately published, 1899).

Thomas Jefferson, *The Writings of Thomas Jefferson* (New York: G.P. Putnam's Sons, 1892-99, Worthington C. Ford., ed., 10 vols.).

Dumas Malone, *Jefferson the Virginian* (Little, Brown and Company, 1948).

" *Jefferson and the Rights of Man* (Little, Brown and Company, 1951).

" *Jefferson and the Ordeal of Liberty* (Boston: Little, Brown and Company, 1962).

Meade Minnigerode, *Jefferson—Friend of France* (New York: G. P. Putnam's Sons, 1928).

Raddin, George Gates, Jr., *Caritat and the Genêt Episode* (Dover, NJ, Dover Advance Press, 1953).

Schminke, Frederick A., *Genêt: The Origins of His Mission to America* (Toulouse: Imprimerie Toulousaine Lion et Fils, 1939).

Harlow Giles Unger, *The French War Against America* (Hoboken, NJ: John Wiley & Sons, 2005).

" *Mr. President: George Washington and the Making of the Nation's Highest Office* (Boston: Da Capo Press, 2013).

Francis Wharton, *The Revolutionary Diplomatic Correspondence of the United States* (Washington, D.C.: Government Printing Office, 1852).

George Washington, *The Papers of George Washington:*

Confederation Series, January, 1784-September, 1788 (Charlottesville, Va.: University Press of Virginia, 1992-1997, 6 vols.).

Presidential Series, September, 1788-May 1793 (Charlottesville, Va.: University Press of Virginia, 1987-1997 , 21 volumes.

Revolutionary War Series, June 1775-April 1778 (Charlottesville, Va., University of Virginia Press, 1984- , multi-volume [in progress],

Periodicals

American Historical Review (1794)
Gazette of the United States
Illinois Historical Society Journal (1928)

Journal of American History\Mississippi Valley Historical Review (1920)

Kentucky Gazette
National Gazette (Philadelphia)

New York Historical Society Quarterly Bulletin (1970)
Revue de l'Histoire de Versailles et de Seine-et-Oise (1925)

Smithsonian Magazine
Virginia Magazine of History (1966)

Reference Works and Manuscript Collections

American State Papers, Foreign Relations (Washington, D.C., 1832).

Annual Report of the American Historical Association for the Year 1903, II.

Bibliothèque de l'Institut de France, Paris.

Bibliothèque Nationale de France, Paris.

Library of Congress, Washington, D.C.

Ministère des Affaires Étrangères [Paris], Archives des Affaires Étrangères, Correspondence Politique, États-Unis.

Notes

[*] Let us fight tyranny; its bloody standard threatens;

[†]Do you hear the roar of ferocious enemy soldiers across the land?

[‡] *The enemy is almost in our midst!*

[§] "Oh, all will be well, will be well, will be well; the aristocrats are on the gallows; Yes, all will be well, will be well, will be well; we're going to hang them all!"

[1] To William Short, January 3, 1793.

[2] TJ To the General Assembly of North Carolina, Washington, January 10, 1808,*The Life and Selected Writings...,*319

[3] *The Correspondence between Citizen Genêt...and the Officers of the Federal Government...Instructions from the Constituted Authorities of France* (Philadelphia: Benjamin Franklin Bache, 1793).

[4] Thomas Jefferson letter to William Short, January 3, 1793, Founders Online; Manuscript Division, Library of Congress.

[5] Gouverneur Morris, Minister to France during the Terror, *A Diary of the French Revolution* (Boston: Houghton, Mifflin Company, 1939, 2 vols., Beatrix Cary Davenport, ed.), I:158-159.

[6] Gouverneur Morris to George Washington [henceforth GW], December 28, 1792; January 6, 1793, *The Papers of George Washington, Presidential Series* (Charlottesville: University of Virginia Press, 21 volumes, 2002, 11: 559-563; 593-594.

[7] Gouverneur Morris, ibid., II:596-596.

[8] Thomas Jefferson to James Madison, May 19, 1793, Founders Online.

[9]. Minnigerode, 221.

[10] Corwin, 41.

[11] Doniol, I:2-4.

[12] Doniol:I:6.

[13] *The Adams Papers, Diary & Autobiography of John Adams,* L.H. Butterfield, ed. (New York: Atheneum, 1961, 4 vols.), IV:246.

[14] (Jonathan Sewell, David McCullough.*John Adams,* 348-350.

[15] Corwin, 277.

[16] Corwin, 275.

[17] Minnegerode, 64-65.

[18] Wharton, 6:48-49.

[19] *Journals of the Continental Congress, 1774-1789* (Washington, D.C., Library of Congress, 198, 34 vols., Worthington Chauncy Ford., ed.), 1:35-37.

[20] Corwin, 413.

[21] Doniol, V: 192.

[22] *Annual Register*, as cited in Corwin, 375-376.

[23] Kaminsky, 169.

[24] Poniatowski, *Talleyrand aux États-Unis*, 350.

[25] Gouverneur Morris to George Washington, December 28, 1792; January 6, 1793

[26] Ammon, 7.

[27] DeConde, *Entangling Alliance*, 181.

[28] Alexander Hamilton, writing pseudonymously as "Pacificus" in *Gazette of the United States*, July 3, 1793.

[29] DeConde, *Entangling Alliance*, 221.

[30] Malone, *Ordeal of Liberty*, 97.

[31] Ibid.

[32] Tobias Lear to George Washington, April 8, 1793, *PGW Presidential Series*, 12:434-438

[33] Memorandum from Thomas Jefferson to the President, July 26, 1793, PGW, *Presidential Series*, 13:287-290.

[34]. *Instructions to Citizen Genêt, Minister Plenipotentiary from the French Republic to the United States, from The Executive Council*, Archives des Affaires Étrangères, Paris, Volume 38,

Dossier Correspondence Consulaire: *Genêt*.

[35]. *Kentucky Gazette* (Lexington), April 5,1794.

[36] Thomas Jefferson to Thomas Mann Randolph, Jr., June 14, 1793, in Ford, VI, 318.

[37] Memorandum from Alexander Hamilton, May 15, 1793, *Papers of George Washington, Presidential Series,* 12:577-584.

[38]. Archives des Affaires Étrangères, Ministère des Affaires Étrangères, Quai d'Orsay, Paris, Volume 38, Dossier *Correspondence Consulaire: Genêt.* {Hereafter: AAE Genêt]

[39] AAE Genêt.

[40] *New York Spectator*, November 16, 1798.

[41] Malone, *Ordeal of Liberty*, 46.

[42]. Richard Harwell, *An Abridgment in one volume of the seven volume George Washington by Douglas Southall Freeman* (New York: Charles Scribner's Sons, 1968), 622.

[43] Harlow Giles Unger, *The Life and Times of Noah Webster* (New York: John Wiley & Sons, 1998, 186.

[44]. Ibid.,71, 183.

[45] Alexander DeConde, *Entangling Alliance* (Durham, N.C.: Duke University Press, 1958), 207.

[46]. [Not until 1856, with the Declaration of Paris, would the world's leading maritime powers

agree to codify the rights of neutrals and belligerents on the high seas. The Hague Conventions of 1908 added further clarification and codification of the rights and obligations of neutrals.]

[47] Minnigerode, 191

[48] Philadelphia *National Gazette*, June 5, 1793.

[49]. Minnigerode, 184.

[50]. AAE Genêt, Volume 38, Dossier *Correspondence Consulaire: Genêt.*

[51]. John Adams to Thomas Jefferson, June 30, 1813, in Lester J. Cappon, ed., *The Adams-Jefferson Letters: The Complete Correspondence Between Thomas Jefferson and Abigail and John Adams* (Chapel Hill: University of North Carolina Press, 1959), 346-347.

[52] Stanley Elkins and Eric McKitrick, *The Age of Federalism: The Early American Republic, 1788-1800* (New York, Oxford University Pres, 1995), 360.

[53] Thomas Jefferson to James Madison, July 7, 1793, Founders Online

[54] *American Daily Advertiser,* August 26, 1793

[55] Malone, *Ordeal of Liberty,* 97.

[56] AAE Genêt.

[57] Without correspondents or other links to major city newspapers, the nation's press copied articles from big-city newspapers to keep readers in smaller constituencies informed. It was an era of "scissors-and-paste journalism," according to historian Henry Ammons, 141.

[58] DeConde, 254.

[59] *New York Spectator*, November 16, 1798.

[60] DeConde, 254.

[61] Ibid., 254-255.

[62] To Thomas Jefferson from Edmond Charles Genêt, May 23, 1793, Founders Online, National Archives.

[63] Thomas Jefferson to Jack Eppes, May 12, 1793, in Dumas Malone, *Jefferson and the Ordeal of Liberty* (Boston: Little, Brown and Company,1962), 81.

[64] Minnigerode, 205.

[65] Malone, *Ordeal of Liberty*, 97.

[66] Thomas Jefferson to James Madison, May 19, 1793. Founders Online.

[67] Malone, *Ordeal of Liberty*, 282-283.

[68] Minnigerode, 208; Ammon, 67.

[69] Ford I: 238-240.

[70]. Ammon, 70.

[71]. Minnigerode, 223.

[72] Memorandum from Alexander Hamilton and Henry Knox, July 8, 1793, PGW, *Presidential Series,* 13:185-191.

[73] Ibid.

[74] Ibid.

[75] Charles Edmond Genêt to George Clinton, September 6, 1793, PPW, *Presidential Series*, 14:48n.

[76] Minnigerode, 223.

[77] Ibid.

[78] *Instructions to Citizen Genêt, Minister Plenipotentiary from the French Republic to the United States, from The Executive Council,* French Foreign Ministry, vol. 38 *Dossier Correspondence Consulaire.*

[79] Minnigerode, 223.

[80] Ford I: 236

[81] Ibid., 265.

[82] Donald H. Stewart, *The Opposition Press of the Federalist Period* (Albany: State Univ. of New York Press, 1969), 132.

[83] Ibid., 312.

[84] AAE-Genêt.

[85] AAE-Genêt. [The French terms "republican" and democrat" were synonymous.]

[86] Genêt to Jefferson, December 20, 1793, *The Correspondence between Citizen Genêt...and the Officers of the Federal Government* (Philadelphia: Benjamin Franklin Bache, 1793).

[87] George Washington to Governor Henry Lee, September 17, 1793, in Carroll and Ashworth, *George Washington*, 131.

[88] Ammon, 97.

[89] Ammon, 97.

[90] Ibid; Minnigerode, 421.

[91] George Washington to Thomas Jefferson, July 25, 1793, Founders Online.

[92] Ibid, 267.

[93] George Washington to Richard Henry Lee, October 24, 1793, Founders Online.

[94] Minnigerode, 210.

[95]. Ibid., 81.

[96]. Minnigerode, 183.

[97]. Henry Ammon, *The Genêt Mission* (New York: W. W. Norton & Company, 1973), 91;

George Washington to Virginia Governor Henry Lee, October 16, 1793, Fitzpatrick, *Writings*, 33:132-133.

[98]. Minnigerode, 282.

[99] Thomas Jefferson to Archibald Stuart, January 4, 1797, in John P. Kaminski, *The Quotable Jefferson* (Princeton, NJ, Princeton University Press, 2006), 435.

[100].GW to Frances Bassett Washington, February 24, 1793, in PGWP 12:264-265.

[101]. Donald H. Stewart, *The Opposition Press of the Federalist Period* (Albany: State University

of New York Press, 1969), 132.

[102]. Ibid., 312.

[103]. AAE Volume 38, Dossier *Correspondence Consulaire: Genêt.*

[104]. *Greenleaf's New York Journal*, August 28, 1793.

[105]. *Boston Columbian Centinel*, August 17, 1793.

[106]. John Adams to Thomas Jefferson, June 30, 1813, Cappon, 346.

[107] *The Diary*, or *Loudon's Register* (New York), August 12, 1793.

[108] *New York Daily Advertiser,* August 6, 1793.

[109] DeConde, *Entangling Alliance*, 288.

[110] Thomas Jefferson to Charles Edmond Genêt, August, 16, 1793, in DeConde, *Entangling Alliance*, 288.

[111] Ammon, 108.

[112] Jefferson to Madison, August 11, 1793, Founders Online.

[113] Thomas Jefferson to James Madison, July 7, 1793, Founders Online.

[114] British Ambassador George Hammond to British Foreign Secretary Lord Grenville, February 22, 1794.

[115] Fauchet to Randolph, February 22, 1794, AAE, Correspondence Consulaire, v. 3.

[116]. John Adams to Abigail Adams, February 23, 1794, cited in Alexander DeConde, *Entangling Alliance*, 398.

[117]. Minnigerode, 362.

[118] John C. Miller, *The Federalist Era* (New York: Harper & Brothers, 1960), 161.

[119] "Letter to Mazzei, in Malone, *Ordeal of Liberty*, 267

[120] Harwell, 701-702.

[121] TJ to John Blair, Paris, August 19, 1787 in John P. Kaminski, ed., *The Quotable Jefferson,* Princeton University Press, Princeton, NJ, 2006, 143.

www.ingramcontent.com/pod-product-compliance
Lightning Source LLC
Chambersburg PA
CBHW051219160726
47994CB00002B/667